The *Greatest* Little Business Book

The Essential Guide to Starting a Small Business

Written by Peter Hingston

Illustrations, cartoons and graphic design by Charlotte Hingston

HMSO   The Inland Revenue, Customs & Excise and National Insurance forms and tables in this book are Crown copyright, reproduced with the permission of the Controller of Her Majesty's Stationery Office.

Note   In the worked examples in this book, all persons, companies and businesses are fictitious.

Important   Although we have tried to ensure the accuracy of information in this book, no responsibility for loss occasioned to any person acting or refraining from action as a result of material in this book can be accepted by the author or publisher. Due to the complexities involved when starting or running a business, we strongly advise the reader to take professional advice before making any decisions.

Suggestions   Although the author welcomes constructive comments or suggestions (some of which have been incorporated in this book), he is not able to handle queries relating to readers' personal business matters. These queries are best referred to a local business development unit, professional adviser or relevant government department.

Copyright © 1998 by Peter Hingston. All rights reserved. 8th Edition.

Previous editions: Copyright © 1985, 1987, 1988, 1990, 1991, 1993, 1995.
Reprinted: 1986, 1987, 1988, 1989, 1992, 1994, 1996, 1997.
Foreign language editions: Polish (1992), Ukrainian (1994), Hungarian (1994).

Published by Hingston Publishing Co.,
Conifer House, 14 Ainslie Close, Hereford HR1 1JH, U.K.
Telephone: 01432 344693   e-mail: hingston.publishing@btinternet.com

Printed in Great Britain by Hobbs the Printers Limited.

ISBN 0 906555 20 5

Introduction

I hope you will find this a most useful book – I only wish there had been such a book when I first started in business! I have tried to write it to be clear, readable and full of practical information.

The first edition was written in 1985 when I was Director of a Local Enterprise Agency providing advice to people setting up in business and I could not find a suitable book for my clients. The book therefore tries to answer precisely the sort of questions people ask when they are thinking of starting a business. It also points out those things which people do not know to ask about, but which they certainly need to know about, if they are going to have any chance of succeeding.

As your time is short, please don't feel you have to read the book from cover to cover, just dip into the section which is of immediate interest.

If you have not already made contact with your local Business Link (in England), Business Shop (in Scotland) or Enterprise Agency (located everywhere in the UK), remember they are there to help you and much of their advice is free.

I wish you every success with your new venture.

P. Higston

Acknowledgements

Charlotte Hingston — For the illustrations, cartoons, suggestions for the text, proof reading and the encouragement necessary to complete this project.

Jimmy Walker — For detailed analysis and comprehensive suggestions for the text.

I am also indebted to the following who read sections, chapters or complete draft manuscripts and who provided many suggestions which were incorporated in the first edition of the book. (Appointments are those held in Summer 1985).

Fred Brooksbank	Scottish Development Agency
Elizabeth Cameron	Inverclyde Enterprise Trust Ltd
Craig Campbell	Arthur Young, Glasgow
John Carpenter	Milton Keynes Business Venture
Robert Colvil	R. W. Colvil & Co
Edward Cunningham	Scottish Development Agency
Eric Firth	Welsh Walker & Co
Tom Ford	Colchester Business Enterprise Agency
Dick Glover	Industrial Relations & Personnel Consultants Ltd
David Hingston	Procurator Fiscal, Wick
John Jacobs	Edinburgh Venture Enterprise Trust
Joanna James	3i, Edinburgh
Don Kennedy	Small Firms Service, Glasgow
David Lochtie	Thomas Bryce Insurance
Roger Massey	Strathclyde Microsystems Centre
Lilian Morris	
George Paterson	Glasgow Opportunities
Mac Robertson	
William Smith	Campbell Smith Insurance
A.J. Stewart	Industry Department for Scotland
George Stewart	Royal Bank of Scotland plc
Jack Thomson	Woodrow & Thomson

My thanks also to Gerry Quigley, Chairman of the Inverclyde Enterprise Trust Ltd in 1985, for his permission to use the Trust's IBM PC computer on which the original text was typed. (The book has been re-typed many times since then).

Additional Acknowledgements for the 4th Edition: Don Kennedy of Business Information Services; Roger Harvey of Willow Typesetting.

Additional Acknowledgements for the 6th Edition: Peter Bevan; Federation of Small Businesses; Irene Goodall; Perth & Kinross Environmental Health Department; Scottish Business Shop; Tayside Trading Standards Department.

Additional Acknowledgements for the 7th Edition: Stuart Ramsden; DTI Press Office (London); Tayside Trading Standards Department; Tayside Fire Brigade (Fire Safety); DSS (Contributions Agency), Perth.

Front Cover Photographs: M. Lungley (Blacksmith); Jean Munro (Whoops A Daisy); Min Clements (Wildtrack).

Contents

Thinking of a Business Idea

THE very first step in setting up a business is to think of what the business is going to do, in other words you need to have a "business idea". You might think this is purely a matter of inspiration with the lucky entrepreneur waking up in the middle of the night with the great idea that will make him or her a millionaire! That might happen on the odd occasion but it is rare.

Getting the right business idea usually requires a good deal of thought and careful research. To find an idea, keep asking yourself "just what is it that people want?" and when you think you have found a suitable idea, ask yourself "will it attract enough customers?".

The lucky entrepreneur waking up in the middle of the night ...

This chapter is for those readers who are thinking of setting up in business but who have not yet thought of what they are going to do. Here are some of the techniques that people use to come up with a business idea:

Copying This is probably the most common way a business idea is conceived. In essence it works like this — you might see a product or service which is not available locally so you could fill the gap by introducing it to your area. Almost every shop is an example of this, but there are many other possible examples — leisure industry activities, local magazines etc.

To get such an idea you could visit another area (if outside London, you can pick up good ideas by a one-week visit to the capital) or better still, if you can afford it, visit the Continent or North America. The last destination is a rich source of business ideas and products which are not yet available in this country — just walk the streets, look around the shops, watch the TV commercials and read the papers and magazines to get lots of ideas. Of course not everything that is a success abroad would necessarily be such a success in this country.

One form of copying that is not usually recommended is to simply mimic an established local business and to set up in direct competition.

Franchising This is similar to "Copying" as mentioned above except you do it with the full support of the business you are copying under an agreement called a "franchise". In this the franchise giver (called the "franchisor") allows you to use his name and get his expertise with all its benefits. In exchange you as the "franchisee" have

to pay the franchisor for the benefit of using his name and obtaining his advice but the major advantage is that it allows the new entrepreneur to get into business more quickly with less of the risks that normally exist. This is an important enough technique to merit a section of its own later in this chapter.

Buying An Existing Business This is another popular means for acquiring a business idea, and in fact, shortcuts much of the start-up process. But its very ease belies the possible pitfalls and many a retired or newly redundant person has lost all his or her money buying a shop, pub, sub-post office or small hotel. It is an important subject and is covered in a separate section later in this chapter.

Product Spin-Off This is where a designer while working on one product might realise that a variant of that product has quite a different use and so he sets up his own business to exploit that. Alternatively he or she might think of a significant improvement to an existing product which, if it was to go into production, would take a good share of the market. (Legal advice may be required to ensure you do not infringe any patents etc).

Arts & Crafts This applies mainly to those with a formal training in arts and crafts or who have some unusually good talent. It must be admitted that trying to start a profitable business based on your arts or crafts talents is very difficult for many complex reasons — one of which is the problem of distributing your product widely enough through many outlets. Again there are exceptions but you have to identify a

Thinking of a Business Idea

real market need which is large enough to provide you with a living wage. You also need to know how to promote and distribute your products and allocate enough time for this in addition to your creative work.

Inventions There is a widespread belief that you have to invent something before you can start a manufacturing business. The fact is that few businesses start this way and though some have been enormously successful it is not an easy path to tread. In Britain only about 2% of patented inventions are now by private individuals, the remainder being filed by companies and government research departments.

One might think the biggest problem is designing the new device but in fact that is the least of it for the main problem is selling it to a generally disbelieving public who are naturally conservative and wary of new things. To launch an innovative product requires substantial promotional or advertising budgets. Also, of every 10 new product ideas only one is ever likely to go into production.

Personal Experience This is often a good way to stumble onto business ideas, a personal experience having revealed a market gap. For instance, you might have difficulty in obtaining say, a book that gives you all the essential advice you need to lay out a new garden and if you find that other people have the same problem then you might consider writing one!

Or, when you are trying to sell something, the customer might reply *"We don't really want that, but what we really need desperately and cannot get is a (something else)"*. This approach

Patents Relate to products, processes, mechanisms, materials etc. To be patentable an invention must be: 1. new; 2. involve an inventive step and 3. be capable of industrial application. Advisable to contact a registered Patent Agent at an early stage (see Yellow Pages).

Registered Designs Relate to the looks or style of a product. Is judged solely by eye. Only the appearance given by an object's actual shape, configuration, pattern or ornament can be protected, not an underlying idea. Again, best to contact a Patent Agent.

Warning: If you wish to apply for a patent or registered design, contact a Patent Agent *before* publicly disclosing your invention (or design) as such disclosure forfeits your protection.

Reg'd Trade & Service Marks Relate to a symbol or word or combination that distinguishes the products (or service) of a particular business. It provides protection for the goodwill and reputation of a firm. Handled by Patent Agent or Trade Mark Agent.

Copyright Relates to printed matter, music, works of art, architecture, films, computer programs etc. 3-D articles now have "Design Right" protection where based on a designer's drawings. In the UK no registration is required but vital to have proof of date. Protection is automatic and immediate. May be advisable to use the copyright symbol © etc.

Note You cannot protect a business idea, only something physical.

often prompts very good sales leads as it reveals what the customer really wants rather than what you thought he wanted. The good salesman would then ask his next customer *"Do you ever need a (whatever)?"* and if the answer is similar to the first customer and confirmed by others then he has probably found a good business idea.

Hobbies/Sports Sometimes there are business opportunities that can arise from your hobby or sport. In this situation, success requires the entrepreneur to have a fair amount of experience in the sport or activity to know what is required. In particular, many good sportsmen and women use their talents to make money outside their sport but related to it. For instance, golf professionals open golf shops. Their experience allows them to know what products to stock, their fame can be used to get publicity for the enterprise and their advice will be appreciated by customers. But a word of caution — some people involved in hobbies or sports dabble in selling something related to their activity but which will earn little more than pin money. There is a risk with this approach to business ideas that people start a business more for their love of the sport or hobby rather than there being a clear market need which they can fill and which will give them a living.

In General

Your business idea will have a better chance of success if you can develop a "unique selling proposition", ie a product or service that customers cannot obtain elsewhere. This does not require the whole business to be unique but you must offer something that is different, which could be the style of your service, the manner in which you package your products etc.

FRANCHISING

A Success Story Statistics which record the failure rate of new businesses vary depending upon the size of companies considered, the number of years before trading ceases and so on, but without any dispute the figures all show a depressing picture. At least one in three of all new small businesses starting this year will not be trading in 3 year's time. Although fair comparative figures are hard to come by, it would appear that franchised new businesses in the UK have a better chance of surviving than the norm.

What Is Franchising? This is when an established business is prepared to licence you to use its product (or service), its image, its name and its business knowledge – in fact the whole proven business format.

For any new business to succeed, it must have: a product or service that is needed, a suitable size of market, the correct stock and tools, adequate finance, appropriate premises and, most importantly, people with the right skills to do the work and who have the necessary "business knowledge" (such as how to do sales and accounts). If any of these factors is weak, the chance of failure increases, so you can see why someone setting up in business for the first time has to get a lot of things right just to survive.

With a franchise, the business you take on should be a well proven business idea and the professionals behind the franchise (called the "franchisors") should be able to provide you (the "franchisee") with all the training and back-up you need to ensure you succeed. They are keen to see you prosper because they take a percentage of your takings (called a "royalty") and so their profitability is directly linked to your profitability. This is good insurance for you as you can be sure that they will maintain their interest in what you are doing!

Who Does Franchising? The type of franchising we are considering here is more correctly called "Business Format Franchising". Developed in the United States in the 1950s, many of the well-known franchise names are still American. In the United States one third of all retailing is done by franchise operations and it is a fast growing sector of the economy. In Britain franchising is becoming more familiar to people and there are now many hundreds of companies operating franchises, including some well-known names.

How Does Franchising Work In Practice? Setting up any business takes money, called "capital". With a franchise operation it costs you more, because you are paying for the business experience and proven product or service of the franchisor. In return he may set up the whole business for you – including the selection of premises, the associated legal work, the full training of yourself and finally, help you with selection of stock and/or tools. In some cases this "hand-holding" is so complete that the franchisor gets the premises completely ready and you are simply handed the keys to your own shop or fast-food outlet. While the premises are being found and prepared, the franchisor will be busy training you to run your new business.

What You Should Get In A Franchise

1. A proven business format.
2. The use of a business name/trademark.
3. The Operations Manual.
4. Training in both "trade" and business skills.
5. An exclusive territory.
6. Full support on start-up.
7. On-going advice and guidance.
8. Long-term market research to ensure your business keeps up with changes in the market place.
9. A contract clearly defining the rights and obligations of both parties.
10. Advertising support.
11. Trouble-shooting.

How To Assess A Franchise Operation

1. Get the franchisee information pack.
2. Visit the franchisor's head office.
3. Visit at least two of their franchisees (of your choice).
4. Assess several different franchises before choosing one.
5. Consult an accountant and solicitor before committing yourself.
6. Ask probing questions, such as:
   When was the business established?
   How many outlets are there in the UK?
   Who are the people behind the franchise?
   How good is the company's financial performance?
   What is the minimum capital required?
   What is the annual royalty charge?
   What do you get for your money?
   Are there other charges, eg advertising?
   What is the long-term for the product or service?
   Who is the competition?

Thinking of a Business Idea

When you start trading there is an Operations Manual which lays down the whole format of how to run the business – it is your "bible". In good franchise operations the franchisor works in close association with you to ensure you make good profits and run a sound business. This is in their interest as they want a royalty, calculated as a fixed weekly or monthly amount or, better still, a percentage (2% to 20%) of your sales. Note this royalty is usually based on your sales figure and not on your profits!

The rights and obligations of both parties are described in a contract which is a detailed document and forms the basis of the close association between yourself and the franchisor. Remember that contract law in Scotland and England are different so use a solicitor local to your area.

How To Find A Suitable Franchise

Many franchisors are members of the British Franchise Association (Thames View, Newtown Rd, Henley-on-Thames RG9 1HG. Tel: 01491 578049). They provide an information pack (currently £25) for prospective franchisees, that includes a list of their members.

In addition, Franchise Development Services (Tel: 01603 620301) publish the *Franchise Magazine* and the annual *UK Franchise Directory*. There is also the *Franchise World Directory*, produced by *Franchise World* magazine (Tel: 0181 767 1371).

To meet franchisors, there are several major franchise Exhibitions held around the country (get details from the British Franchise Association).

FURTHER READING

There is a also a good book: *Taking Up A Franchise* written by Colin Barrow and Godfrey Golzen, which is published by Kogan Page.

A Parting Shot

If you want to start your own business and (a) do not know what to do, (b) have a reasonable amount of capital, say £5,000 minimum and (c) are not a loner who resents anyone being involved in your venture, then becoming a franchisee is one way to get into business. Prior experience of the trade that the franchise involves is usually not a requirement as franchisors prefer to instill their own methods during the training phase. Many successful franchisees are ex-executives or ex-forces personnel. A word of caution: taking on a franchise does not guarantee success as some have failed whilst others fail to meet projected turn-over figures. Even if successful, it will require much hard work and time for the business to become established.

Although there are certain constraints on being a franchisee such as you cannot adapt or modify the business or introduce sidelines, an important aspect of being in business for yourself, ie the amount of profit you can make, is mainly in your own hands.

KEY POINT Always consult both an accountant and a solicitor before signing anything!

BUYING AN EXISTING BUSINESS

This is a popular way for people to get into business for the first time and it can be successful, as it short-cuts much of the difficult start-up process. You may hear about businesses for sale by word of mouth. They are also advertised in local newspapers and the publications: *Businesses & Premises For Sale* and *Daltons Weekly* (from newsagents). Shop sales are also handled by Business Transfer Agents (see Yellow Pages).

The Second-Hand Car Syndrome

Have you ever seen a second-hand car gleaming in some showroom and felt you just had to own it, only to drive it home and discover it had so many faults you wished you had never seen it? Well, many people on being presented with the opportunity to buy over another person's business often suffer the same experience so I have called it affectionately the "second-hand car syndrome". In the context of this book it might work something like this . . . .

Mr Smith was made redundant in his 50s but one day, while talking to the owner of his local newsagent/general store, he learned that the store was up for sale as a going concern and he was flattered that the existing proprietor was prepared to offer the shop to him. Already the second-hand car syndrome was beginning to take effect as Mr Smith rushed home to tell his wife about the fantastic offer he had just been made. Mrs Smith was not so sure as she knew the store was never busy when she was there, it was always out of things she needed and the interior was a bit tatty. When she mentioned that to her husband he dismissed it saying that with some money spent on it he could increase the turnover "easily". Mrs Smith asked quietly if Mr Smith had asked the proprietor why he might be selling to which her husband replied the reason was due to ill health. Mrs Smith was unconvinced as she was thinking about the effect of the large supermarket that had been opened recently just a few streets away.

One hopes that Mr Smith took good professional advice from a surveyor and an accountant and indeed heeded their advice which was probably that the proprietor was now selling as the business was declining due to the competition of the new supermarket. How can you stop yourself falling into the same trap? The answer is to do your homework thoroughly, to look carefully at the accounts, and to maintain an open yet cynical mind.

Why cynical? Because one must examine why a good small business is being sold. If the business is doing even reasonably well it is more likely to be taken over by a close friend, a member of the proprietor's family, or the proprietor could employ a manager. That is not to say that good or potentially good businesses do not come onto the market but the parallel to second-hand cars is close ... you need to know fully about what you are taking on and why it is being sold.

to put you in touch with a similar business probably far enough away not to be in direct competition. You will be surprised how many people will be quite happy to speak to you and impart good advice and hints. Also visit the local library and ask the librarian if there are any books on the subject, as many different types of business now have books written about them, sometimes written by people who have had to learn the hard way.

What Will It Cost? This is not an easy question to answer as every business has its own strengths and weaknesses. However, in general terms a business has value due to its:

Stock This is best valued independently (ie not by the seller). Remember all businesses suffer from "dead" stock

take into account their depreciated value.

Note: Depreciation is an accounting term which tries to put a life on an item. For instance, if the likely lifetime of a machine is 4 years, its value "depreciates" by 25% each year so if it cost £100 new, after a year its "accounts book" value would be £75, and after two years its value would be £75 less 25% and so on.

Machinery & Equipment This is valued like Fixtures & Fittings.

Goodwill Whereas the above categories can be valued precisely (it can still lead to disputes), goodwill is the really "grey" area of valuation. Goodwill equals the value of the Business less the tangible Business assets. It is a measure of the momentum of profitability that the business has built up. It should therefore be based on the proven profit of the business, looking at the last few years (since the business may be growing rapidly or declining). If a typical net profit (before tax) figure can be agreed on then the goodwill can be valued for a small business at usually between 1 and 5 times the profit figure. The actual multiplier chosen is dependent upon all the other factors involved in the sale, ie the perceived growth potential of the business, any patents or designs owned by the former business, the quality of staff and their training and the size of the existing customer base. Goodwill is very negotiable and if it relates closely to the former owner that part will be lost when he or she leaves and in that case it would be worth less!

The total value of the business, ie what you have to pay, is the sum of the four factors above of which the last is the most negotiable. Interestingly, the

Buying a business can be like buying a second-hand car.

Trade Knowledge Do you know anything about the trade or the business you are contemplating taking over? If not, you are very vulnerable! Contact your local Enterprise Agency or business development unit (see the chapter **Getting more Business Advice**) for their advice and ask them

which is stock that is unlikely ever to be sold as it is either out-of-date, damaged or was never saleable in the first place! The valuation should therefore be the depreciated cost price (not retail price) of the saleable goods.

Fixtures & Fittings Again this should be valued independently and it should

Thinking of a Business Idea

larger the business the greater the multiplier used when calculating the goodwill.

Note that if the goodwill is, for instance, 3 x net profit of the business, then it will take you three years just to recoup that money, and that assumes the business continues to generate the same profits.

Financial Aspects Get advice from an accountant, who should go through the last few years accounts of the business and explain to you all the salient features. Be sure you also understand any tax implications of the purchase and you may also need to read a copy of the VAT publication: *Transfer of a Business as a Going Concern*.

Existing Staff Look carefully at the terms, conditions and rates of pay for existing staff as you have to observe these. Are the wages paid realistic? If you plan to reduce the number of staff you could be liable for redundancy payments. See the **Employing Staff** chapter.

Market Research A big advantage of buying over an existing business is that you have access to real trading figures gleaned from the accounts of the business, so you can make better cash-flow and profit predictions. But trading conditions vary constantly and you must still do thorough market research to ensure that market conditions are not likely to vary adversely for the foreseeable future.

Premises Most businesses operate from an office, shop or factory. If you are contemplating taking over a business it is therefore imperative to enquire fully into the situation regarding the premises. Are the premises owned by the company or rented? If they are rented then how long is the lease for, are there restrictions on the use of the premises, how much is the rent, when is there a rent review and does the landlord have to approve any new tenant? Check the lease carefully. It is essential for a structural survey to be done and for you to find out if you would be responsible for the repairs and insurance of the building. The surveyor can also comment on the lease prior to you consulting your solicitor. See the chapter **Finding Premises**.

Limited Companies If the business you are buying is a limited company, you first need excellent legal advice, because when you take on a company (usually by the purchase of a majority of its shares) you not only take on the assets, but also ALL its liabilities, which might be substantial. Be warned!

BUYING AN EXISTING BUSINESS

If you want to buy an existing business:

1. Get the facts: details of stock, fixtures & fittings, machinery & equipment, staff; what value the owners place on the business; up-to-date accounts for the last 3 or 5 years; copy of the lease (if premises are rented).

2. Do thorough Market Research, as described in the next chapter.

3. Prepare a Business Plan and raise the finance, as described later.

4. Get good professional advice. This is absolutely vital.

5. Do not sign anything until the above steps have been completed and, just like buying a second-hand car, do not be hurried into a decision by the seller saying other buyers are interested or that he (or she) must have your offer within a few days.

KEY POINT **There Are Many Ways To Make £££** There are many ways to make a living, but the lifestyle can vary enormously and this should be taken into account at this stage before you are saddled with debt, leases, stock, staff and so on. For instance, if you choose to open a small general store/newsagent, then you can expect to work a 7-day week with a very early start to the day. Shops in general have large stock, onerous leases (if rented) and often have staffing problems. But at least it is a cash business, ie your customers do not expect any credit. In contrast, many manufacturing concerns suffer from customers who take many months to pay (or never do!) and the business usually has to operate on small margins – but at least you can close the door and go home on a Friday evening (even if you still take some of the paperwork home).

Some service businesses have the advantage of requiring little stock and have low overheads, but are frequently the type of business that is copied readily by competitors (or it may be the type of business where your customers expect you to answer the phone when they have a problem even at 9pm in the evening!).

These lifestyle aspects do need full consideration as they will be with you for the lifetime of your business■

BEFORE STARTING

Chapters

Doing the Market Research

THIS chapter is to help you answer the fundamental question: "Is there a market for my product (or service) and is it likely to be big enough to support me and my business?"

Finding the answer requires what is called "market research". If you start a business, almost any business, you will always be able to make some sales but what you really need to find out is will you be able to sell enough to make even a modest living? Frequently would-be entrepreneurs say "I'm not trying to make a lot of money, just enough to live on". But what they may not realise is that just to make enough money to survive might require more sales and success than they had anticipated. Here is a specific example ...

Assume you want to manufacture a car accessory which you plan to sell through car accessory shops. This particular product, called a SAYIT, attaches to the rear of a vehicle and when the driver wants to flash a message to the vehicle behind he merely operates a switch on the dashboard and the SAYIT lights up the word "Thanks" or "Sorry" as appropriate (or maybe something a little stronger!). The material cost in the device is approximately £5 and if it is wholesaled to the car accessory shops for £6 then the gross profit per unit will be £1. How many units do you think you need to sell to make the equivalent of a £6,000 wage? Is it 6000, 8000 or 10000?

It is not 6000 as you might suppose as you have other costs, called "overheads" to pay for, such as workshop rent/rates, telephone calls, postage, travel etc which may add up to £4,000 per year (or more). So to make £6,000 per year you will have to make and sell 10000 SAYITs. The question your market research must answer is "Will the market buy 10000 SAYITs per year at a wholesale price of £6?" Note that if 10000 SAYITs are likely to swamp the market then you will do little trade in your second year!

Market research can be thought of in 3 parts:

1. **Analysis of the market.**
2. **Analysis of competitors.**
3. **Testing the market** (before you fully commit yourself).

ANALYSIS OF THE MARKET

This gives you an inside picture of the trade you are thinking of entering, the trends both nationally and locally and an understanding of the needs of your potential customers. It is achieved as follows ...

The National Situation Many industries are described fully in market research studies carried out by organisations such as Mintel and Key Note and copies of their reports are available at large public libraries. You might also notice articles in newspapers or on television which refer to trends. Beware though of the "Media Bubble", where excessive coverage is given in the press and on TV to a new craze or trend. If one is to believe the media there appears to be a huge market and often dozens of firms will pop up in response but it is unlikely that the actual market size is large enough, or that the demand (if it existed in the first place) will be sustained.

Even if your proposed business does not need a national-sized market to sustain it, national trends can have a significant effect at a local level. You need to know if the industry you are entering is expanding, contracting, stable or very dependent upon another industry which itself is changing rapidly. There may even be legislation in the pipeline that could have a major effect on your plans.

Knowing trends has another significance, because those people who get on to the "band-wagon" of a new product or service early on often do much better than those who come along later, but of course the early entrepreneurs are exposed to greater risk. Good examples here are laundrettes and video hire shops, where the first people into the new market did very well indeed.

Other sources of market research information are trade magazines, trade associations and their exhibitions. Your local library should be able to give you the names of trade magazines (from a directory called BRAD) and they should also be able to help you locate the appropriate trade associations.

The Local Situation Once you have some knowledge of the national situation and relevant trends you need to know much more about the trade on a more local level. To this end there is no better source of information than the trade itself! First of all speak to the sales representatives of your likely suppliers – they can provide good information if asked the correct questions. They are, after all, trying to engage your interest in their products so they should talk, reminisce and tell you their business problems if gently encouraged. This will build you up an interesting picture.

Next, through the assistance of your local Enterprise Agency or business development unit try to meet someone doing the same business in a different

Doing the Market Research

part of the town or county (so that you would not be in direct competition). You will be surprised how helpful most people can be.

KEY POINT Before you meet anyone, always write down the questions to ask. Take a note of their answers.

The Target Market   This is the phrase used to describe that section of the population that could potentially use your product or service and is therefore your "target". For your business to succeed you need customers (that's obvious isn't it?) but have you stopped to think just who those people are and what exactly their needs are and what benefit they will get from using your product or service? They are obviously surviving without you at present so why will they want to use your business? Also, are there enough potential customers within reach of your business?

Before proceeding further you need to be clear as to whether you will be selling to trade customers, the general public or both. There are major differences between the two, for instance trade customers generally have larger budgets and different requirements, such as the design of the packaging, when goods are to be delivered or the date by which work must be completed. Another major difference is that trade customers expect credit – at least 30 days, sometimes much more, whereas a private customer is prepared to pay immediately.

This whole matter of credit can have fundamental implications for a new business as providing credit (or receiving credit from trade suppliers) can have a marked effect on your cashflow, and

giving credit costs you money and can lead to bad debts. Cashflows are discussed in a later chapter.

Trade Customers   To do the market research, first prepare a list of all the companies who you believe may be interested in your product or service. Get their names from the Yellow Pages or a Trade Directory. You then need to contact them to find out their views on what you have to offer. Before you make such an approach you will need to know what your prices will be (see chapter **Marketing And Sales**). The technique then is to get an appointment, either by phoning first or writing a letter (see the example on page 73).

Private Customers   If you are selling to the general public, trying to find out who will buy what from you is much more difficult than with trade customers. In this case try to start by asking people already in the trade as their customers are likely to be similar to yours. The next step is to speak directly to likely customers and the most thorough way of doing that with the general public is to use a questionnaire – see the end of this chapter.

KEY POINT There is no substitute for actually talking to your potential buyers and it is best done before you are committed to the project.

ANALYSIS OF COMPETITORS

A great deal of interesting and useful information can be derived from close observation of potential competitors. To locate competitors:

1. Consult the Yellow Pages and any Trade/Business Directory.

2. If your intended business is retail – walk the streets in the area where you are thinking of setting up and mark on a street plan the name and location of competitors.

3. Ask your suppliers' sales reps who else they supply in your area.

Checking-out the Competition
A number of techniques are possible:

1. Sit outside your competitors' premises (sit in a nearby café or in a car) and observe the people or vehicles

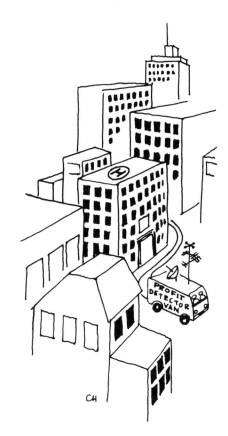

A number of techniques are possible....

coming and going. Take notes. This can reveal: In the case of shops – how many people go in and how many come out with purchases. In the case of factories – the names of suppliers and customers (conveniently written on the sides of vans or lorries) and the general level of activity of the business, ie quiet or busy. This observation needs to be done at several different times of the day or week and for an hour or more at a time.

2. If a competitor is a limited company, they have to file annual accounts and annual returns. These are available to the general public for a small fee. They give the names of Directors and financial details. For those companies registered in England or Wales these details are available by post, by phone (tel: 01222 380801) or by visiting: Companies House, Crown Way, Maindy, Cardiff CF4 3UZ. Tel: 01222 388588. Alternatively you can visit Companies House, 55-71 City Road, London EC1, tel: 0171-253 9393.

For companies registered in Scotland, these details are available by post, by phone or by visiting: Companies House, 37 Castle Terrace, Edinburgh EH1 2EB. Tel: 0131-535 5800.

There are also Satellite Offices in Birmingham, Manchester, Leeds and Glasgow.

For companies registered in Northern Ireland, these details are available from: Companies Registry, IDB House, 64 Chichester Street, Belfast BT1 4JX. Tel: 01232 234488.

3. If the competitor is a manufacturer, try to buy, rent or borrow a sample of their product and check it out noting strengths and weaknesses. How does it compare with your own product? Note too any patent markings.

4. If the competitor is in the service sector try to use their service or if that is not possible ask friends to phone as if they were customers and get them to ask about prices and how soon they can get the service (as this may reveal how busy your competitors are). This same technique could be used for manufacturers if data on their products is hard to acquire.

5. Obtain pamphlets, sales literature and price lists whenever available, by writing, phoning or at trade shows where the competitor has a stand.

6. If possible, try to speak to past or present customers – this can often be most revealing.

KEY POINT   Keep a file on each competitor enclosing all the information you have built up on them.

Assessing The Situation   Once you have completed the above market research (which may take several weeks or much longer), you will need to sit back and assess the situation. In particular you should by this stage be able to estimate if your proposed business venture will either increase the likely size of the market (most common with new products or services) or will it succeed only at the expense of your competitors? Sometimes it is a mixture of both, but the implications can be significant.

If you think you will be expanding the market it means new customers will be using you – where will they be coming from and what is it that attracts them? Are you expecting them to stop buying something to have the spare money to spend it with you?

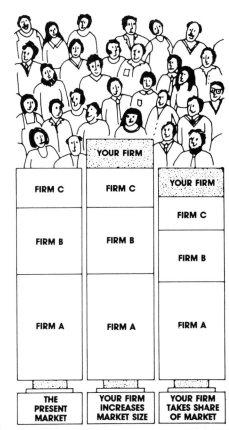

MARKET SHARE

Alternatively if you are trying to "muscle into" an existing market how will you win customers from other suppliers? One way is to offer a better quality product or service. But when you start trading, there is a serious danger of counter-attack from existing businesses as they will not simply open the door to you. In contrast they are much more likely to slam the door in your face. Such door-slamming techniques could include – dropping their prices to

Doing the Market Research

engage you in a price war, poaching your key staff by offering higher wages or interfering with your sources of supply. In any event you would be unlikely to win unless you have enormous resources behind you, so it is worth thinking about and should never be underestimated.

TESTING THE MARKET

This is not always necessary but it can be very useful where the other market research carried out is rather inconclusive. Test marketing is sometimes called "flying a kite" or "putting a toe in the water" and that helps to explain what it is about. Its function is simply to test the market reaction to a new product or service with the minimum of investment and is usually done at an early stage before one is fully committed to the project. It is a very common practice and takes a number of forms:

The Advert   This is the simplest way to check the market though it has limitations (see chapter **Marketing and Sales**). With this form of test marketing you advertise a product or service as if it were actually available (even if you are not quite at that stage) to see what reaction it produces. But note your advert must not be misleading.

The Sample   If it is a product you are making which is to be sold to the trade you take samples to potential customers and take orders before committing yourself to full production. This practice is common in the fashion and gift trades.

The Mailshot   In this case you send a letter to any potential customer

requesting a response which would indicate their interest in what you have to offer. This can be a very effective technique especially if the customers are businesses and the letters are addressed to named individuals or appropriate posts (see the example on page 73).

The Leaflet Drop   A version of the mailshot but less personal and best suited for the general public by slipping the leaflets through their letter boxes. It can also be used for trade customers or could be inserted into newspapers or magazines (called "inserts").

The Exhibition/Trade Show   Yet another way to judge market reaction to your product or service is to rent a stand at a suitable exhibition or trade show. It is useful because unlike all the above options (except **The Sample**) you get immediate feedback from potential customers. This can be crucial in helping you to fine tune your product or service, establish prices etc. Note that participating in exhibitions can be very costly in terms of cash and time. Also, the success of them should be judged on the contacts made and not necessarily the amount of business done on site.

In Conclusion   In most test marketing an element of bluff is essential, particularly if you have not yet commenced trading and are trying out the market before you commit yourself. Since nobody particularly wants to deal with a "business" that is just starting or operating from a garden shed (or worse!), the use of first, a business name and second, a trade address could be beneficial though not essential. Trading under a business name is

easy (see chapter **Making it Legal**) but finding a trade address could present more of a problem.

AND FINALLY ...

The market research you will have to do forms a fundamental part of the Business Plan which comes after the next chapter in this book. Many people think that market research is only done before starting a business or launching a new product or service. In fact

---

10 Common Errors When Doing Market Research

1. Speaking to everyone except the actual potential buyers.
2. Failing to notice warning signals as you are convinced your project will work.
3. Asking "loaded" questions, the answers to which just confirm your ideas without revealing the interviewee's thoughts.
4. Ignoring the fact that often 20% of the customers provide 80% of the turnover.
5. Assuming you will compete effectively just because your prices will be lower.
6. Being influenced by your contacts who promise to supply you with lots of work when you start. (Ask yourself how they are getting by without you now, and ask your contacts for more details of their needs to test their genuineness).
7. Underestimating how long it can take to enter a market and take a reasonable market share (it's years, not months).
8. Failing to recognise the strength and the reaction of the competition.
9. Basing your likely sales estimates on the simple assumption that you will take x% of the total market.
10. Forgetting that new products or ideas take time and money to introduce to the market. (People are very conservative).

market research should be thought of as an on-going activity and is covered further in the later chapter **Marketing and Sales**. When you start trading remember to follow up the sales leads and potential jobs you found when doing the market research.

QUESTIONNAIRES

The first way to get an idea of people's needs in a general sense is to read market research reports (as mentioned earlier). However, those are usually researched on a national scale. To find out more about the needs, views and habits of local consumers, you need to ask them and this is best done using a questionnaire. The 5 golden rules of questionnaires are:

* Keep it short and simple.
* Do not "load" the questions.
* Do not ask "open" questions.
* Ask likely customers.
* Ask as many people as you can.

Keeping It Short And Simple Ask yourself, what is it you are trying to find out. Ask only the most important questions and avoid any fringe issues. There should be no more than 5 to 10 questions. A multiple choice or Yes/No format is best as it is both easier to answer and quicker to analyse.

"Loaded" Questions If you were considering buying a mobile shop then you might ask householders in the appropriate district as to their views to assess if the business would be viable. A question such as "Do you buy anything from a mobile shop at present?" would be a reasonable question but if you were to ask "Would you use a mobile shop if it was cheaper?" invites

Mobile shops? ... Yes, yes, all the time ... convenient, ... my mother did too... near my last home ... very handsome driver and nice beef. Now let me see ... what time of day? Out most mornings ... evenings are best ... bridge on Mondays with Mrs Whosit, ... Tuesdays are my new cookery course ....

Do not ask "open" questions.

the answer "yes" without much consideration as it is a "loaded" question. In this case it may be more useful to ask the householders what time of day they were at home so you could plan your round. It is very easy to fall into the trap of asking "loaded" questions. Try to avoid emotive or exaggerated phrases in the question. Also, be aware that people often naturally give the reply which they think you want to hear.

"Open" Questions The purpose of the questionnaire is to find out precise answers to specific questions so you

can draw conclusions. The danger of "open" questions such as "Do you think mobile shops are a good idea?" is that it could lead to a long debate! Instead, to each question on the questionnaire the answer should be either yes/no or one answer of a multiple choice. In general, avoid asking for people's opinions, stick to the facts. (As your experience increases, you can try a more open question as sometimes they can be most revealing).

Ask The Right People To get the right people might involve house-to-house interviews or if doing the survey in the main street stop only those people who you think might use your product or service. There may be places that your likely customers congregate. For instance if you were planning to set up a business selling sports equipment obviously you would visit local gyms, local athletics clubs etc. Remember you do not need the name of the person you are interviewing.

Ask Many People Within reason the more people you ask the more accurate will be your survey. To make the analysis of the survey data easier you could type out one questionnaire and photocopy it so that with each person you ask, you complete a new sheet. This makes adding up the figures at the end easier. You should ask at least 100 people, maybe many more if possible■

Making it Legal

ONCE you have completed your market research, the next step is to prepare a Business Plan, but before you can do that, it is necessary to digress briefly to look at some of the legalities involved when setting up a business.

CAUTION Please note this chapter is for general guidance only and should not be regarded as a complete or authoritative statement of the law. For more information, please consult a solicitor or the relevant authorities.

Sole Trader/Partnership/Limited Company or Co-operative? An early decision is what legal form the business should take. If you are going to be a one-boss business you could be a "sole trader" (ie self-employed) or a "limited company" while if there is going to be several "bosses" you need to be a "partnership", "limited company" or "co-operative". Some people think that they must form a limited company when they start in business but this is not necessarily the case.

Sole Trader This is probably the most common form when a business starts. You can trade under your own name or a business name (see below). You can also employ staff. Should the business fail owing money, then your creditors can seize your personal possessions to recover their losses. Many businesses start as "sole trader" but as they grow they usually change to a "limited company" status for two reasons: a) the limited liability protection of their personal possessions and b) it is easier for them to raise larger sums of money for expansion.

Partnership If two or more people work together and no-one is an "employee" then the law regards the arrangement as a "partnership", which has important consequences. Most importantly, each partner will be "jointly and severally liable" for any debts the business runs up. What this means in practice is if Partner A buys a car using a business cheque which subsequently bounces, the car dealer can pursue Partner B for the entire amount! Also, unless there is an agreement to the contrary, profits in a partnership have to be shared equally between partners.

It is a sad truth that many partners come to blows but this could be avoided if the partners started off with a good written Partnership Agreement.

It is a sad truth that many partners come to blows.

See the example at the end of the chapter — roughly draft your own agreement based on this and then see a solicitor and an accountant. There are many complex issues involved and you will need proper advice. You may not need all the clauses listed in the example or you may even like to add new clauses.

If, due to personal circumstances, the partners contribute different amounts of capital then they can choose to either: a) apportion the profits in the same ratio as the amounts invested or b) allow time, say 6 months, for the partners to equalise their investments to allow the profits to be shared equally. In both cases voting rights should be equal as well as personal drawings.

Choose your partner(s) carefully. They could lead to your personal bankruptcy just as easily as helping you to make a profit. It may be better for them to be employees rather than partners. Finally, remember to take out "cross insurance" which is a life assurance policy payable to the other partner(s) in the event of a partner dying to enable the surviving partner(s) to purchase the deceased partner's share of the business from his estate and to continue trading.

Limited Company Unlike a sole trader a limited liability company is a legal entity in its own right. Its shareholders and Directors may change but the company will continue to exist until wound up. Companies have many laws to regulate them and no-one should consider setting up a company without fully understanding the implications and having taken professional advice. A limited company used to require a minimum of two shareholders (who could be husband and wife) but since 1992, Single Member Companies have been permitted. A company must have at least one Director. The company must also have a company secretary who could be a second Director, another shareholder or your accountant or solicitor.

Companies House (addresses on page 17) produce a series of free small booklets which give more advice and are highly recommended reading.

Directors derive benefits by being paid an employee's salary or fees while shareholders get paid "dividends" out of the profits. One can buy an "off-the-shelf" company for around £150-£200 and this can be done within days. Only buy from a reputable company to ensure what you are buying is indeed a "clean" company without liabilities. Contact your solicitor or look under "Company Registration Agents" in the Yellow Pages. Winding up a company,

---

The Choice: Limited Company or Sole Trader/Partnership?

Advantages of Ltd Co: Limited liability of shareholders (ie should the company fail, in most cases all you would lose is your share capital); easier to raise larger sums of money; easier format to cope with investors who do not want to work in the business; greater credibility.

Disadvantages of Ltd Co: Wages of Directors are subject to PAYE; higher annual accountancy charges; overall taxation maybe greater due to high National Insurance contributions; public disclosure of some key data; cannot offset losses against your previous income tax.

You can buy an "off the shelf" company.

in contrast, can be much more expensive and protracted.

Co-operative A co-operative can be thought of as a specialised form of limited company. Here we are referring to "workers' co-operatives" rather than the high street shop groups that also use this name. Co-operatives are run like any other small business with managers or supervisors, the difference being that the business is owned by everyone who works in it and any decisions are made democratically.

Workers' co-operatives are still quite rare in the United Kingdom. Get further information from ICOM (the Industrial Common Ownership Movement) at: Vassalli House, 20 Central Rd, Leeds LS1 6DE, tel: 01132 461738.

In Scotland, contact Employee Ownership Scotland (tel: 0141-554 3797) and in Wales, the Wales Co-operative Development and Training Centre (tel: 01222 554955).

Business Names

A sole trader can trade under his own name (married name if a woman) ie as William Smith, W. Smith, Wm. Smith, Smith or William David Smith and a partnership can trade under the names of all the partners. But if a business name is to be used (eg "Smith's Giftshop") then the requirements of the Business Names Act 1985 apply. The Act prevents you from using certain words in a business name and regulates the disclosure of business ownership (as detailed below).

Sensitive Words You cannot use any name for your business – it must not be offensive and the use of certain words needs approval, eg Limited (unless you are incorporated), International, National, British, Scottish, Irish, English, Welsh, European, Royal, Group, Trust, Society, Breeder, Registered etc. A list of such words and how you might get permission to use them is given in the booklets "Business Names and Business Ownership" and "Sensitive Words And Expressions" available from any Companies House.

Note that as there is no registration of business names, someone else might unintentionally use the same name unless you formed a limited company (as no two companies can have exactly the same name).

Making it Legal

Disclosure of Ownership The Business Names Act also requires:

1. Business Stationery All letterheads, orders, invoices, receipts, statements and demands must carry in addition to the business name, the names of all the owners and in relation to each person named an address "at which documents can be served" (normally the business address). Refer also to the letterheads illustrated on page 62.

2. Business Premises Sign This same information must be displayed prominently and legibly on a sign in all the places where you carry on your business and deal with customers or suppliers. There are no set rules as to the design of this sign but one suggestion is illustrated below. Note that the size of the sign should be commensurate with its surroundings.

3. On Request The names and the addresses of all owners of the business has to be given immediately in writing when requested by any supplier, customer or other person with whom the business has dealings.

Companies: The Business Names Act also applies to any company that uses a trading name other than its own, eg if "ABC Foods (XYZ) Ltd" wishes to trade simply as "ABC Foods".

In addition, the Companies Act requires a company to paint or affix its name on the *outside* of every office or place where it carries on business.

See also the free Companies House booklet *Choosing a Company Name*.

Note there are special rules for Welsh companies.

Licences/Registration You can start most businesses right away as there is no need for registration or licensing, but there are important exceptions, some examples being:

Selling tobacco or alcohol; providing driving instruction; operating an employment agency; child minding; scrap metal dealing or processing; providing public entertainment; night-clubs; massage; dealing in second-hand goods; operating as a street trader or mobile shop; driving a taxi or private hire car; operating certain goods and passenger vehicles; cleaning windows; hair-dressing; selling door-to-door; residential care and nursing homes; betting and gaming; most activities relating to pets or animals; providing credit services (and debt collecting, hiring, leasing etc – refer to the "Consumer Credit Act" on page 24). Also, if you are going to sell or handle food you must speak to the Environmental Health Department at a very early stage of the project (and before you start trading).

The list above is only a sample and failure to obtain a licence or register may be a criminal offence.

KEY POINT Contact your local Council, Business Link or Business Shop to find out if your project needs a licence or other approval.

PARTICULARS OF OWNERSHIP
of

SIMPLY PERFECT

as required by the Business Names Act 1985

Full Name(s) of Owner(s)	Address at which Documents can be served
Miss Joan Smith	12, Regent Crescent Greenock PA1 1ZZ

An example of a sign, completed with fictitious particulars

INSURANCES

Where applicable, it is a legal requirement to have vehicle insurance, certain engineering insurances and employers liability insurance. It would be prudent to be adequately insured for other risks so you should discuss your proposed venture with an insurance broker (who should be a registered broker).

The broker may only be able to give you an estimate at this early stage as you probably will not have the full details they require. The various types of insurance which you may consider are covered below:

Employers Liability This is a legal requirement only if you employ someone and then the certificate has to be prominently displayed at the place of work. It is not required by sole-traders (or partnerships) with no employees. This insurance is to protect employers against claims for damages, brought by employees for death or bodily injury sustained in the course of employment (which includes injury caused by other employees for whom you are liable).

Public Liability This provides you with protection against claims for which you may be legally liable brought by anyone other than employees for bodily injury or loss or damage to property arising in the course of your business. It also covers the legal costs incurred when defending such claims.

Product Liability This provides protection for legal liability for claims arising from injury, loss or damage due to products you have sold, supplied, repaired, serviced or tested. It can be expensive.

Professional Indemnity This is for anyone who wants to start a business as a consultant (legal, management, technical, marketing, financial etc). This insurance protects you against your legal liability to compensate third parties who have sustained some injury, loss or damage due to your own professional negligence or that of your employees.

Vehicles You must, of course, carry motor insurance but if you intend to use your car or van in the business, check that your insurance covers you (and any other driver) for the commercial purpose you propose. Generally for a car there will be an additional premium for using it in connection with your business.

Goods In Transit As a rule, motor insurance policies do not cover goods being carried in the vehicle so if you intend to carry goods you may need this additional insurance cover.

Premises If you are buying premises or it is a condition of the lease that you should insure the premises, then you should be covered against fire and special perils (eg burst pipes, storms, malicious damage). Check too that your plate glass windows (where relevant) are covered. Your insurance broker will advise you if it is necessary to be covered for "Property Owners Liability" as this risk may already be covered by the Public Liability policy.

Stock, Fixtures & Fittings, Plant and Machinery Be careful not to underestimate the value of these. Note that if your cover is for "reinstatement value" it provides for the full replacement cost while "indemnity value" is the current market value less depreciation (which can be significant!). Insurance should cover losses due to theft, vandalism, fire, flood etc. Accidental damage or "all risks" cover can also be arranged in many cases if so required.

Engineering If the business has plant or machinery which must have a periodic statutory inspection then it is usual to arrange for this to be done by a specialist engineering insurer under an inspection contract, with or without insurance cover on the plant or the machinery.

Money If your business involves handling cash in significant amounts then insurance cover against theft would be prudent. Policies normally cover loss of money in the premises and also money in transit to or from the bank. If covered for cash in transit be sure to comply with the small print.

Once your business is established you may also want to consider:

Employment Protection When you are employing people, particularly if it is a large number, the complex employment legislation which covers employees rights, unfair dismissal, redundancies and so on can cripple a small company both financially and in management time when things start to go wrong. This insurance covers not only legal fees but can also cover personnel advisory services that you will need.

Fidelity Guarantee & Internal Theft This insurance provides protection against dishonesty or theft by members of your own staff.

Consequential Loss If your office, shop or factory is put out of commission due to fire or any other insured peril then this insurance will maintain the financial position of the company as if the calamity had not occurred. Such insurance can be expensive but

Making it Legal

failure to have it can in certain circumstances close a business down permanently when such a disaster occurs.

Personal Health/Life and Pensions

It is wise to consider Personal Health Insurance cover for yourself to provide you with an income should you be unable to work. This is a very important matter and should not be overlooked. Similarly, if the company is very dependent upon one or two key people it may be wise to insure these people against death, accident or sickness for the business may suffer financially in the event of their death or prolonged absence from work.

As the company's fortunes increase you should also consider life assurance and pensions for yourself and perhaps for your staff. This is a complex area that needs good professional advice.

Finally, remember that the services of an insurance broker are free as he or she is paid commission by the insurance companies. A good broker will not try to sell you insurance you do not require but at the same time will be concerned that you do not under-insure. It is a balancing act to a certain extent as you should take out as much insurance as you need, but no more and no less – and in any event you should review the position at least once a year to take into account changes in your business.

LEGISLATION

There are many laws that may affect you when you run a business. Here is a brief guide to just some of the more important laws (listed in alphabetical order). Other laws are mentioned elsewhere in this book, in the appropriate chapters. Be sure to consult a solicitor to find out all the laws and regulations that may apply to your own business.

Consumer Credit Act   In most cases if you are going to provide credit, arrange credit or HP or if you are going to hire equipment for more than 3 months, then you are likely to need a licence under this Act.

You may not need a licence if, for instance, you are simply accepting payment by credit card or you are simply allowing customers to pay their bills at the end of the week, month or whatever period you work to (this includes normal "trade" credit).

The Act is complex and it is a criminal offence to give credit without a licence unless the exceptions such as mentioned above apply. Contact your local Trading Standards Department for more information.

Consumer Protection Act   This Act's main functions are to ensure the safety of goods sold and it also makes it a criminal offence to give consumers a misleading price indication about goods or services. Contact your local Trading Standards Department for more information.

Data Protection Act If you are going to keep information about people on a computer, even if it is just names and addresses, then you need to become registered (costs currently £75 for 3 years). For a form and further information contact the Registrar's Enquiry Service on tel: 01625 545745.

Financial Services Act   This Act requires any person involved in the provision of financial advice, or related services, to register.

Food Safety Act & other Regulations
There are stringent rules regarding most aspects of handling, preparing and selling food. For instance, equipment, premises, food handlers, storage, working methods, labelling etc are all covered. Speak to your local Environmental Health Department at the very start of your project.

Trade Descriptions Act   This Act requires traders to use correct descriptions of their goods and services.

Unfair Terms In Consumer Contracts Regulations   This applies to all terms in a contract (including pre-printed terms on order forms and invoices) where you are supplying goods or services to a consumer. "Small print" that is deemed unfair will not be binding.

Weights & Measures Act   This Act applies to anyone selling foods, drinks, toilet preparations etc.

Remember: These are just some of the general laws and regulations that may affect you but you need to know all those that affect your specific business.

TAX

First, get a copy of the free government leaflet CWL1, entitled: *Starting your own business?* as it tells you what to do and includes the forms you need.

Inland Revenue (Tax, PAYE)

As a sole trader or partner you do not pay PAYE (Pay-As-You-Earn) income

An Executive Agency
of the Department
of Social Security

Inland Revenue

HM Customs & Excise

For official use only

When completed, return form to **Contributions Agency
Self Employment Group
Longbenton
Newcastle upon Tyne
NE98 1YX.**

The Contributions Agency will send a copy of the completed form to the Inland Revenue, and Customs and Excise.

Use this form to tell the Contributions Agency, the Inland Revenue, and Customs and Excise that you have started self-employment.

It is not a Value Added Tax (VAT) registration form. If after reading the VAT information in this leaflet, you think you are required, or need to be registered for VAT please put a 'X' in this box.

Notification of Self Employment

Yourself

Your title *(for example, Mr/Mrs/ Miss/ Ms)* and current surname

Previous surname *(for example, your surname before you married)*

Your first name(s)

SPECIMEN

	Day	Month	Year
Your date of birth *(in figures)*			19

Your home address

Postcode

Your home phone number *(include STD code)*

	Letters	Numbers	Numbers	Numbers	Letter
Your National Insurance number					

Your marital status – *put 'X' in relevant box*

Single ☐   Married ☐   Widowed ☐

Separated ☐   Divorced ☐

Tax Office to which you sent your last Tax Return

Reference in that Tax Office

Your business

	Day	Month	Year
1 When did you start in business or when will you start?			19

2   What sort of self employed work do you do / will you do?

If you are working in the fishing industry as a share fisherman put 'X' in this box ☐

Your business continued

3   What is your business name and address?

Postcode

Your business phone number *(include STD code)*

Your business fax number *(include STD code)*

4   What is your position in the business? *For example, owner, partner. If you are a subcontractor, put 'subcontractor'.*

5   Do you have any business partners?
Put 'X' in the relevant box   No ☐   Yes ☐

If you have answered 'No', please go to question 6.
If you have answered 'Yes', please state

Partner's full name

Partner's address

Postcode

	Letters	Numbers	Numbers	Numbers	Letter
His/her National Insurance number *(if known)*					

If you have more than one partner, please give details on a separate sheet.

6   How do you wish to pay your Class 2 National Insurance contributions? *Put 'X' in the relevant box*
• by quarterly bill ☐
• by direct debit – *complete the attached application form CA5601 and send it with this form.* ☐

Do you want more information about exception from liability because of low earnings or deferment?
If so, put 'X' in the relevant box
• exception from liability because of low earnings ☐
• deferment (if you are both employed and self employed) ☐

CWF 1   BMSD 3/97   *Please turn over*

Form CWF1 (One side only shown here, reduced in size).   A Contributions Agency, Inland Revenue and H.M. Customs & Excise form. Crown Copyright. Reproduced with the permission of the Controller of HMSO.

Making it Legal

tax, which employees have to pay. Instead you pay income tax on the profits of the business.

 KEY POINT When you start trading you must notify your local Tax Office without delay.

Notify the Tax Office using the form CWF1 (illustrated on page 25), which is provided inside the leaflet CWL1 mentioned on the previous page. If you are going to incorporate a limited company, you need a different form.

If you are going to employ people, you have to operate PAYE. Remember that if you are a limited company with salaried Directors you will also have to operate PAYE. Contact your local Tax Office (look under "Inland Revenue" in the Phone Book) and ask for a *New Employers Starter Pack*.

 KEY POINT If you employ anyone, you must contact your PAYE office without delay.

National Insurance

As a sole trader or partner you will normally have to pay a Class 2 contribution and your business will have to pay a Class 4 contribution if your profits and gains exceed a certain figure. If your self-employed earnings are likely to be small, you can apply to your local Contributions Agency (DSS) office for a "Small Earnings Exception", (see also the **Tax Data Page**).

 KEY POINT When you start trading as a sole trader or partnership, notify the Contributions Agency without delay.

If you are at present in work as an employee paying a Class 1 National Insurance stamp, then if you start a business you will normally have to pay

a Class 2 stamp in addition.

Visit your local Contributions Agency (DSS) office and ask for copies of their leaflets on self-employment. You could also discuss with them how your proposed business will affect any social security benefits you may be receiving.

You can elect to pay your Class 2 contributions monthly by direct debit, the form being included in the CWL1 leaflet mentioned above.

If you form a limited company, as a paid Director you will normally need to pay Class 1 contributions, not Class 2. In addition, the company has to pay an "employer's National Insurance contribution". These are both payable to the Inland Revenue along with your PAYE.

Customs & Excise (VAT)

Value Added Tax (VAT) is a tax on most business transactions, including importing goods and some imported services. With few exceptions you will need to register for VAT if, at the end of any month, the total value of the "taxable supplies" you have made in the past 12 months, or less, exceeds the VAT registration threshold. For the current threshold, see the **Tax Data Page**.

Registration is also required if at any time there are reasonable grounds for believing that the value of the taxable supplies you will make in the next 30 days will exceed the threshold.

"Taxable supplies" are all your sales (other than those that are "exempt supplies", as described below).

 KEY POINT If your turnover meets the VAT registration criteria, you must contact Customs & Excise without delay.

For VAT purposes, all business transactions come under one of three

categories, as follows:

Exempt Supplies This applies to only those very few types of business transaction which are specified as "exempt" from VAT. No VAT is payable and you cannot be VAT registered if you only make exempt supplies.

Zero Rated This applies to only those types of business which are specified as "zero-rated" for VAT. The current list of zero-rated goods (which may change at any time) includes: young children's clothing and footwear, books, newspapers, public transport and basic foodstuffs (but not catering). No VAT is payable. If your turnover exceeds the threshold, you need to register and then you can recover any VAT on business expenses but there is no need to add VAT to your sales (as they are zero-rated). You could instead choose to apply for exemption from registration if your taxable supplies are mainly or wholly zero-rated.

Standard Rated This rate applies to almost all other business transactions. If your business falls into this category and your turnover has exceeded the VAT threshold you must register for VAT. You must then add VAT to your prices but you can recover the VAT you are charged by your suppliers.

To register for VAT, contact your local Customs & Excise Office. See under "Customs & Excise" in the Phone Book. Refer also to the chapter **Coping with Taxation**.

VAT is a complex tax, but the free VAT booklet *Should I Be Registered for VAT?* is easy to read and essential reading for any business. It also includes a VAT Registration Application Form and notes on how to complete it ∎

PARTNERSHIP AGREEMENT

(Note: This is a fictitious example to show you what a Partnership Agreement might look like. The details are of course relevant only to this specific example. Your own agreement should be produced by your solicitor and reflect your own particular circumstances).

We, the undersigned, herein after known as Tring-A-Ling Alarms, and intending to work together in business, agree to the following terms of Partnership:

1. <u>Nature of Business</u>.   The business will be the supply, installation and maintenance of security equipment, and such other business as may be agreed by all the partners.

2. <u>Location of Business</u>.   The business will be located at 10 Sellers Lane, London EC1, and at such other place or places as may be agreed by all the partners.

3. <u>Date of Commencement</u>[1]   The partnership will commence on 1st May 1990 with the partners sharing equal responsibility and liability.

4. <u>Initial Capital</u>.   Each partner undertakes to provide at the date of commencement the sum of £5,000 (Five Thousand Pounds). They further agree not to remove the said sum without the consent of all partners.

5. <u>Role of Partners</u>[2]   All partners undertake to work full time and give their best endeavours to the furtherance of the business. The partners will not undertake other paid or unpaid employment or self-employment or be associated with any other business during the period of this Agreement. No partner without the consent of the other partner(s) shall enter into or terminate any contract for the purchase of goods or services exceeding £1,000, offer employment to any person or terminate the employment of any staff, nor enter into or terminate any property lease arrangements, nor lend any property or assets of the business[3].

6. <u>Voting Rights & Arbitration</u>.   All decisions pertaining to the business will require the approval of all partners. In the event of disagreement, arbitration will be undertaken by the firm's appointed accountant[4].

7. <u>Bank Account</u>.   A bank account in the name of the business is to be opened at the Anytown Branch of the XYZ Bank plc. Thereafter any partner can draw cheques for routine business expenditure up to a maximum of £100. Cheques drawn for amounts in excess of that figure require the signature of two partners. All other documents require the signature of all partners. All cheques and monies received on account of the business are to be paid into the partnership account on receipt.

8. <u>Profits & Losses</u>.   Profits and losses will be divided equally. The partnership will appoint a qualified Chartered Accountant who will prepare the business accounts annually within 60 days of the end of the Tax Year. Goodwill is to be disregarded when

8. (cont'd) computing profits. The partnership books are normally to be kept at the place of business.

9. <u>Drawings & Expenses</u>.   The partners may each draw up to £120 per week. Should there be insufficient funds to meet these drawings, the amount will automatically reduce to that which the funds can meet. The amount is to be reviewed each January. Should any partner elect to leave his drawings in the business he shall be entitled to interest at the current Bank Base Rate and payable quarterly in arrears on the average amount left in the business bank account over that quarter. In addition each partner can draw expenses to cover expenditure on motor fuel but only if incurred in connection with the business and to a maximum of £1000 per annum[5].

10. <u>Holidays</u>.   After six months have elapsed, each partner may take up to three weeks paid annual holiday, the dates of which are to be agreed by all partners.

11. <u>Incapacity</u>.   If in the event of illness or accident a partner is unable to perform his duties his rights and benefits remain intact for three months. Thereafter the remaining partner(s) may elect to expel the incapacitated partner without further notice by sending a letter of intent, by recorded delivery, to his last known address. The procedure for paying out the incapacitated partner is then (as given at Clause 13 below).

12. <u>Admission of New Partners</u>.   Before any new partner is admitted all partners must agree as to first, the capital the new partner should introduce to the business and second, what rights and benefits he or she should enjoy.

13. <u>Retirement[6] of Partners</u>.   A partner may retire from the partnership at any time by giving three months notice in writing sent to the business address. The retired partner's share shall pass to the continuing partner(s) on the date of retirement. The retiring partner is entitled to an equal share of the business assets, excluding goodwill[7], as valued by the firm's accountants by reference to a balance sheet made up to the date of retirement. This share is to be paid in cash to the retiring partner in four equal parts payable, without interest, on the following anniversaries of the date of retirement, namely three months, six months, nine months and twelve months.

14. <u>Dissolution of Partnership[8]</u>   The partnership may be dissolved by agreement of all the partners. In the event of dissolution, all equipment, stock and other assets owned by the partnership are to be sold and the proceeds divided equally after all debts have been settled to the satisfaction of the firm's accountants.

15. <u>Death</u>.   It is expressly agreed that in the event of death of a partner the partnership will continue. In the event of death of a partner during the currency of this Agreement then the deceased partner's share shall pass to the remaining partner(s) on the date of

15. (cont'd) such death. The estate of the deceased partner is entitled to a proportionate share of the business assets, excluding goodwill, as valued by the firm's accountants by reference to a balance sheet made up to the date of such death. This share is to be paid in cash to the deceased's estate in four equal parts payable, without interest, on the following anniversaries of the date of such death, namely one month, three months, six months and twelve months.

16. <u>Income Tax</u>.   Each partner binds himself and his executors to sign if called upon to do so by the remaining partner(s), an election under the Income and Corporation Taxes Act 1988, or any re-enactment thereof, to have the profits of the business assessed to Income Tax on a continuation basis as if no change in the partnership had taken place.

17. <u>Unfair Competition</u>.   (See Note No[9]).

Signatures of all Partners, Witnesses, Date and Place[10].

Author's Notes

(1) Some Agreements also state the duration for which the Agreement is to last, though such a clause would also usually allow the partners to extend the period.

(2) Where one partner is a "sleeping partner", this Clause would obviously need adjusting.

(3) It is difficult to guard against all reckless acts by individual partners which can create friction, but the items listed here are common problem areas.

(4) Alternatively you could refer to the local President of the Chamber of Commerce to nominate an arbitrator.

(5) With expenses it is wise to state an upper limit per annum. Other expenses such as business phone calls made from home may also be covered here.

(6) Many partnerships collapse when a partner chooses to leave demanding his share immediately. It is an important clause therefore and should embrace: a) an independent valuation of the business and b) payments phased over a period that is both fair to the outgoing partner and affordable by the remaining partners. The timescales for payments might be much longer than given in this example.

(7) In my opinion when a business is valued in this context,

"goodwill" should be excluded for the following reasons: a) any goodwill the business has built up has already been enjoyed by the outgoing partner by way of shared profits, b) the outgoing partner may have been the main factor behind any goodwill the business has built up and with his departure will reduce or disappear and c) it is a difficult aspect to quantify.

(8) A Partnership Agreement may also include a clause that allows the expulsion of one partner under certain specified circumstances.

(9) It is a good idea to incorporate an "Unfair Competition" clause in the Agreement if you are concerned that your partner(s) may leave the business at some time in the future and set up in competition with you. However, the wording of such a clause can be tricky and it cannot attempt to prevent a person from earning a livelihood.

(10) The witnesses are merely witnessing the signatures of the partners, they do not need to see the contents of the Agreement. It is better if they witness all partners signing. Note that Scots Law and English Law differ in respect of the requirements for signing and witnessing.

(General) If one or more of the partners are women then the provisions that apply to maternity leave and profit sharing during her absence ought to be included in the Agreement.

Preparing the Business Plan

ONE of the first steps in starting any new business should be the preparation of a Business Plan. What is a "Business Plan" you might ask? It is a planning document which sets out in both words and figures a proposed business venture. This can either be a new business start-up or a major expansion/diversification of an existing business. The need for a Business Plan is as relevant to the business that only requires £1,000 to set up as to the business that needs £1 million.

A Business Plan should be drafted by the people behind the venture – with appropriate advice and help from an accountant and possibly their local Enterprise Agency or business development unit. There is a worked example later in this chapter for a fictitious shop, which we have called "Simply Perfect".

The purposes of any Business Plan are to:

1. **Transfer your thoughts to paper.**
2. **Raise finance.**
3. **Monitor the project.**

We now look at these in more detail . . .

Transferring Thoughts To Paper

When you start a business project there are many aspects to consider. Some are conflicting, while other aspects might be influenced by a casual remark. By putting down the whole business idea in a structured, organised plan the situation should be clarified and you can assess the project more objectively. Furthermore, to complete the plan you have to answer a lot of questions and this forces you to go out and do the necessary research, which is in itself an excellent discipline.

Raising Finance   The Business Plan is the key to open the financier's coffers.

A Business Plan is written in a way that can be understood by financiers and bank managers and is laid out in the sort of format that they are used to. The document should be persuasive, conveying your enthusiasm for the project. Even if you are not planning to borrow money to get your business started, the preparation of a Business Plan could save you losing your own funds.

Monitoring The Project   The Plan lays down the path along which the business should be moving. When a business is started there are so many things to do and in all the rushing here and there it is very easy to delude yourself that the business is doing well just because you are busy. With the Business Plan at your side, you can take stock of the situation, at least monthly, and check to see if you are still moving along the planned path (particularly in terms of the Cashflow Forecast). If not, remedial action can be taken and the sooner the better. Cashflow Management is discussed in more detail in the chapter **Controlling The Finances.**

FORMAT OF THE PLAN

A Business Plan can be laid out in a number of different formats though the information contained is similar. Here one popular format is suggested. Later in this chapter is an example. Your own Business Plan may have longer or shorter sections than the example to tailor it to your own project.

When writing the Business Plan, avoid using too many salesman's adjectives – so phrases such as . . . "the wonderful new product . . ." or "this truly amazing service . . ." should be rationed to keep the plan convincing.

It's a marvelous business idea Which simply cannot go wrong, But the profits galore Which we'll make, I'm sure, Need a loan to help them along!

BANK AGER

Avoid too many salesman's adjectives!

With the example, you will notice there is a cover sheet, several pages of text (typed, never handwritten) followed by a Cashflow Forecast. The same model of Business Plan can be used for any business venture, with larger projects adding a Projected Balance Sheet and other information.

In some cases the Business Plan needs supporting documentation which can be bound within the same covers or simply attached. For instance, you might enclose sales literature. In technical projects, the Business Plan would need to include data covering design, production matters and enclosing relevant drawings, charts and photos.

Preparing the Business Plan

In many larger projects an independent market research report is necessary to give credibility to the plan and again this would be attached to the Business Plan and cross-referred to in the text.

GENERAL POINTS

The whole document should be crisp, neat and free from speling erors!?

In terms of the text, it is usually written in the third person (eg "the Directors" or, as in the case of the example, "Miss Smith"). In contrast, existing businesses may use the first person plural, ie "we". In either case the text should be written with a reader in mind who has never met you and does not know anything about you, your business and maybe even your town, so spell out everything. The Business Plan should emphasise the four key aspects which financial backers look for: evidence of *market research, planning, financial control* and the *competence* of the people behind the project.

THE BUSINESS PLAN CONTENTS

The Cover Sheet   The cover should give a professional look to the document. It gives the name(s) of the people behind the project, the business name and address of the business (or your home address if you do not yet have business premises) and sometimes the name and address of your accountants if they have been closely involved in the preparation of the Business Plan.

Summary   This is a summary of the plan which allows the reader to sum it up at a glance. The larger the plan the more useful is this section.

Contents   A Business Plan with more than, say, 10 pages should have a list of Contents with page numbers so the reader can locate a specific topic quickly. Our worked example omits this as it is quite a short Plan.

Introduction   This is where you make a clear statement outlining the business project and its objectives. Usually one or two paragraphs suffice. If several phases are envisaged this should be mentioned. If a purpose of writing the Business Plan is to raise finance, this should be clearly stated.

Business History   This section is only included where you are buying over an existing business or the Business Plan is by an existing company that is planning a major expansion or diversification.

In this section you would cover the following: the date the business started (usually the date of incorporation if a limited company) and a note of any major recent events in the business's history. You would also state the main products or services, markets, and the particular strengths that have made the business successful.

In addition this section would have a statement on the company's present financial position and would refer to the latest accounts (which would be enclosed at the back of the Business Plan). For larger projects the last 3 years accounts may be required.

Personnel:
Management   This section gives the credentials of the proprietor(s) or Director(s), providing details of their age, qualifications, personal means (eg property ownership), other business connections and most importantly, any relevant experience. For a major project, complete curricula vitae may be required (enclosed with the Plan).

If it is intended to recruit senior staff, eg a Sales Manager, a statement would be made here to that effect.

For anyone embarking on his or her first business it is hoped they would attend a business course and in this section you could make a comment to that effect. In addition if the proprietor(s) are receiving advice and support from a business development unit it is also useful to mention that here. All this is very important as financial backers are as concerned about the *people* they back as their *projects.*

Staff   This part requires a statement on the staff you will need: how many, with what skills, the likely wages you would have to pay, full-time or part-time and what training would be necessary. In some cases this section might indicate a phased increase as the business grows.

Product (or Service):
Description   This section describes in some detail the product or service your business will be offering.

For a product that is to be manufactured, you need to mention its present stage of development. If it is already in production, when was it first launched and how many have been made?. A photo or two, rather than a technical drawing, at the back of the plan, may help the reader's understanding.

In the case of a service business, in this section you would specify precisely what the service is and for what types of customers you are hoping to attract.

Market Research & Marketing Plan   This is a most important section which in most cases should take at least a page of text and in larger projects, much more. Many businesses start with

Preparing the Business Plan

a good product or service but find there are simply not enough willing customers, with inevitable results for the business. It is therefore vital that before any venture goes ahead adequate market research is carried out.

This section in the Plan therefore summarises the findings of the market research and specifically tries to answer the following questions: a) how large is the market for your product or service and what assumptions are you making to arrive at the figures you present? b) what competition is there – with names, details? c) what advantages do these competitors have? and d) what advantages do you have over your competitors, ie what makes you so special? All statements need to be backed up with figures gleaned from the market research. Remarks such as "There is a huge market for . . ." without providing figures are simply worthless.

This section should also outline the Marketing Plan, ie how you propose to advertise, promote, distribute and sell your product or service. To cover this aspect fully may in itself take a page or many more, and should answer the following questions: a) how will your product or service be promoted (with full details and costs), b) how will your product or service be sold, ie by retail, wholesale, agent, mail-order, export or whatever? and c) any planned phases of your marketing operation.

Suppliers & Sub-contractors   Many businesses rely on other businesses to supply them with their raw materials, stock, parts or services. Any problems in obtaining these can spell disaster for a venture, particularly a new one.

Be careful of "single-sourcing" which is when you rely heavily on just one supplier. If possible you should have alternative suppliers. This section of the Business Plan details which suppliers and sub-contractors you plan to use and comments on your discussions and correspondence with them.

Premises & Equipment:

Premises   This section states the type of premises required (ie office, shop, warehouse, workshop, yard, factory etc) and the floor area necessary (usually in square feet). It also states the desired geographic location of the premises (giving reasons) and other requirements such as large loading bays, concrete floors, three-phase power etc. If premises have already been found, this should be mentioned. It should also be stated whether the premises will be bought or rented and if it is expected that the premises will benefit from any special financial assistance.

Equipment   This section of the Plan notes what equipment is necessary, whether it will be purchased new or second-hand and from what source(s). Particularly where the equipment is expensive or extensive, it may be useful to list the equipment needed in an Appendix at the back of the Business Plan. You should also state whether the equipment is to be purchased outright or leased and if any special financial assistance is likely.

Transport   Any van or car will often represent a significant proportion of the start-up and running costs. It therefore merits a statement describing what type of vehicle is required and what its function will be. Do you plan to acquire the vehicle new or second-hand, buy or lease it and what will be its likely annual mileage (which will be reflected in the costs shown in the Cashflow Forecast).

Legal Aspects:

Licence   You would only include this paragraph if a licence was required to carry out the proposed venture and if so from whom such a licence is obtained, at what cost, what time delays are likely and what criteria have to be met before you can obtain such a licence.

Planning Permission   Again you would only include this paragraph if it was relevant, in which case comments should be made on any likely time delay, what criteria have to be met and discussions to date with the relevant planning authority.

Patents   Where relevant this important aspect should be mentioned, in particular what stage you are at in the patent application process.

General   Any laws or regulations that might have a significant effect on the business should be mentioned here together with a comment as to what effect they have or could have.

Financial:

Pricing   This section specifies how you will price your product or service. Retailers, wholesalers and importers should mention their proposed "mark-up". Other service businesses should mention their proposed hourly rates. Manufacturers should mention their "mark-up" or "margin".

$$\text{Mark-up} = \frac{(\text{selling price} - \text{cost price})}{\text{cost price}} \times 100\%$$

$$\text{Margin} = \frac{(\text{selling price} - \text{cost price})}{\text{selling price}} \times 100\%$$

It is usual to mention the norms of your industry. The prices you use are crucial, especially as new businesses often under-price, with dire results.

Preparing the Business Plan

Cashflow Forecast   In some respects this could be classed as the "heart" of the Business Plan as it illustrates in figures, much of what the plan discusses in words.

The Cashflow Forecast is just what it says – a forecast of cash flowing in and out of the business (on a monthly basis). This is normally for 12 months ahead (though a project with long lead times may need a 24 or 36 month forecast).

The preparation of the Cashflow Forecast requires: a) estimates and assumptions which should be clearly stated in the text and b) hard facts derived from your research.

Any grants or other financial help should be noted here. If the one-off start-up costs are significant, as in the worked example, these should be listed in a separate Appendix at the back of the Business Plan.

The golden rule with any Cashflow Forecast is to be pessimistic and not to underestimate your overheads which always seem to become larger than anticipated. Also, it takes time for a business to establish itself and therefore the monthly sales figures should reflect this (with any seasonal variations, such as high Christmas sales, superimposed).

How to do a Cashflow Forecast is covered over the page.

Projected P & L   (Profit & Loss Account). This is also called a "Forecast Profit & Loss Account" or abbreviated to a "Forecast P & L". It would normally be prepared by your accountant and be attached near the end of the Business Plan. It is an important summary as it indicates the likely overheads the business will face and the profit it should make.

Projected Balance Sheet   This lists the projected assets and liabilities of the business and is required for any larger project.

Project Risk Assessment   Every venture has risk but this must be quantified wherever possible. You must assess the risk and equally any potential backer will be interested to know this as their money is at stake.

Potential risk could come from a number of sources – a new competitor, changes in legislation, difficulties in obtaining stock or raw materials, changes in overseas conditions and foreign currency exchange fluctuations, sickness, a bad fire or a flood . . . A more mundane (and common) risk is simply the expected level of turnover is not achieved.

A useful exercise is to do a second Cashflow Forecast assuming 20% (or 50%) less sales while the "overheads" (ie wages, rent, rates, heat, light, phone etc) all remain the same. This could be commented upon in this section with the new (low sales) Cashflow Forecast attached as an Appendix at the end of the Plan. You should also in this section comment on any contingency plans you have to meet setbacks such as who would take over if you became ill.

Financial Requirements   This is usually the last paragraph and it should state in clear unequivocal terms the total money the project needs, how much you are putting in and if any loans are required. Loan requirements should be split into share capital (for a limited company), bank loans and overdraft facilities, and when this money is required. In addition you should state in broad terms what the borrowed money is to be used for.

Appendices   These are found at the back of the Business Plan. Appendices can include:

Cashflow Forecast . . . essential.

Forecast P&L . . . desirable for small projects, essential for others.

Projected Balance Sheet . . . ditto.

Trading Accounts . . . only if taking over a firm or expanding yours.

Technical Data . . . as appropriate.

Market Research . . . where done independently or if lengthy.

Sales Literature, Leaflets, Photos, Diagrams . . . where available.

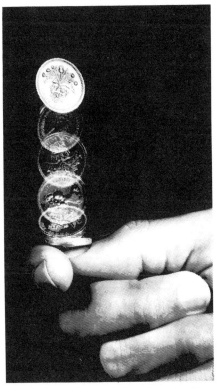

Don't just trust to luck – plan ahead!

Preparing the Business Plan – Cashflow Forecast

	CASH IN												TOTALS
1	Sales (inc VAT)												
2	Bank or other Loans												
3	Owner's Capital												
4	Other Money In												
5	TOTAL												
	CASH OUT (inc VAT)												
6	Stock/Raw Materials												
7	Advertising & Promotion												
8	Bank Charges/Interest												
9	Business Insurance												
10	Drawings/Salaries/NI												
11	Electric/Gas/Heat												
12	Fees (eg Accountant, Lawyer)												
13	HP/Lease/Loan Payments												
14	Motor – Fuel												
15	– Other Expenses												
16	Postage/Carriage												
17	Rent & Rates												
18	Repairs & Maintenance												
19	Staff Wages												
20	Staff PAYE/NI												
21	Stationery/Printing												
22	Sundries												
23	Telephone/Fax												
24	Travelling												
25	VAT												
26	Other Expenses												
27	CAPITAL EXPENDITURE												
28	TOTAL												
29	Net Cashflow												
30	Opening Balance												
31	CLOSING BALANCE												

CASHFLOW FORECAST

This section refers to the blank Cashflow Forecast (left) and the worked example Cashflow Forecast on page 44 – note that each vertical column represents one month and glancing down the left side the lines are numbered 1 to 31.

Cashflow Line Headings

The horizontal lines 1 to 4 list all cash "IN" (ie all the money paid in or received by the business) and lines 6 to 27 list all cash "OUT" (ie purchases and expenses paid by the business). Note these line headings are not rigid, use those appropriate to your own venture.

Top Line: Thirteen columns – one per month for a year, plus "TOTALS".

Line 1 (SALES (inc VAT)): In this crucial line you have to estimate your likely sales (called "turnover") for the year ahead. The assumptions you make should be stated in the text of the Business Plan.

With almost all businesses you have to build up your trade and so there should be a gradual build-up from a low monthly sales figure to a plateau which can be anywhere from months 6-18 for a shop or a year or much more if it is a manufacturing business with long lead-times. There could also be seasonal variations.

If you are offering credit, you should show the payments in the month when you expect to *receive* the cash.

One of the most common errors people make when completing their first Cashflow Forecast is that they wildly over-estimate their likely sales.

Break-even In a situation where it is almost impossible to forecast your sales, then you could do a "break-even" cashflow, ie you would complete the whole cashflow form leaving the SALES line until the very end and then you insert what SALES you have to make to break-even (in practical terms this means ensuring the bottom line of the cashflow remains positive or within your overdraft limit).

Line 2 (LOANS): This line is for bank loans or loans from other sources.

Line 3 (OWNERS CAPITAL): This is for the capital you put into the business.

Line 4 (OTHER MONEY IN): This is for any grants or a VAT repayment.

Line 5 (TOTAL): This equals the total of cashflow line numbers: $1+2+3+4$.

Line 6 (STOCK/RAW MATERIALS): Here you list the value of the stock or materials you have to buy (including VAT). In many cases there will be an initial "stocking-up" phase and then this line should bear a relationship to the SALES line as you cannot make sales without stock! If you get 30 days credit from your suppliers, this can have a marked bearing on your cashflow. Try it yourself and notice that with, say 30 days credit, your own cash needs to set up a business are reduced.

Line 7 (ADVERTISING & PROMOTION): Here is listed any expenditure on adverts and promotion.

Line 8 (BANK CHARGES & INTEREST): Bank charges are often quarterly and vary greatly depending on your usage of your bank account. If your cashflow shows an overdraft requirement, to get a quick (and approximate) estimate of interest charges, take the interest as 1% per month, so in our example where the overdraft for the first three months is: -£1,150, -£1,505 and -£1,709, then the quarterly interest charge is approx: £11.50 + £15.05 + £17.09 = £44.

Line 9 (BUSINESS INSURANCE): The sample shows this as £350.

Line 10 (DRAWINGS/SALARIES/NI): This is for your "Drawings", ie the "wages" you (and any partners) take from the business. For a Director, this is called a "salary". Include here also any National Insurance (NI) contributions and PAYE.

Line 11 (ELECTRIC/GAS/HEAT): This line is for any energy bills. Check with your local supplier as to how often they issue their bills, eg quarterly.

Line 12 (FEES): This line is for any legal, accountancy or other fees (eg surveyor).

Line 13 (HP/LEASE/LOAN REPAYMENTS): This line is for HP or Lease payments if you are buying vehicles or equipment on HP or leasing them. The line is also for loan repayments and so is related directly to line 2. Smaller bank loans are repaid by fixed monthly payments over several years. If you need a bank loan, ask your bank for loan repayment figures so you can complete this line.

Line 14 (MOTOR – FUEL): This is separated from other motoring expenses as it can sometimes be useful to account for fuel usage separately.

Line 15 (MOTOR – OTHER EXPENSES): eg servicing, repairs, annual tax disc and insurance.

Line 16 (POSTAGE/CARRIAGE). This is for post, parcels and courier services.

Line 17 (RENT & RATES): Most business rents are paid monthly or quarterly in advance, and most councils allow rates payments over a number of months as shown in the example.

Preparing the Business Plan – Cashflow Forecast

Line 18 (REPAIRS & MAINTENANCE): This line is for repairs to your premises and equipment (vehicles are covered on line 15).

Line 19 (STAFF WAGES): This line is for all wages you pay to your staff.

Line 20 (STAFF PAYE/NI): Put all staff PAYE and National Insurance payments on this line. (Note your own PAYE/NI contributions appear on line 10).

Line 21 (STATIONERY/PRINTING): For any stationery, printing letterheads etc.

Line 22 (SUNDRIES): This is for all the little bits you will find you need!

Line 23 (TELEPHONE/FAX): For a phone line you may need to pay a "connection charge" plus rental in advance. Put any mobile phone costs on this line too.

Line 24 (TRAVELLING): This is for costs incurred while travelling in the course of doing your business (eg on sales trips or attending trade shows or meetings away from your office).

Line 25 (VAT): A small business may not need to register for VAT unless its turnover exceeds the current threshold figure (see the **Tax Data Page** at the end of this book). In the worked example, the fictitious shop "Simply Perfect" has not registered for VAT as its projected first year's turnover is less than the current VAT registration threshold. So line 25 remains zero.

For a VAT registered business, line 25 is used for the VAT payments made to HM Customs & Excise.

Line 26 (OTHER EXPENSES): This line is for any expenses which do not come under the categories listed above. You may wish to have several such lines on your own Cashflow.

Line 27 (CAPITAL EXPENDITURE): This "capital expenditure" covers once-off purchases of tangible assets such as vehicles, machinery, tools, office equipment, buildings (including alterations) etc. They tend to have a big effect on your cashflow but since the timing of such purchases are under your control, the Cashflow Forecast can help you decide when to make a purchase.

Line 28 (TOTAL): This totals lines 6 to 27 and represents the total cash outflow for each month.

Line 29 (NET CASHFLOW): This is line 5 less line 28. If the figure is positive it means that more cash was received than was spent during the month – that's good. If negative, more cash was spent than received – that's not so good!

Line 30 (OPENING BALANCE): This always starts at 0 for a new business, and each month equals the CLOSING BALANCE of the previous month.

Line 31 (CLOSING BALANCE): This is the sum of lines 29 and 30 and it represents the forecast cash in the bank at the end of each month – which is of singular importance! If this line is negative, it means your bank account is overdrawn and you need an overdraft.

Important Note: The bottom line of a Cashflow Forecast represents neither a "profit" nor a "loss", so don't let that confuse you. But it is worth noting that if you can keep the bottom line *positive,* you will not run out of cash and the business should therefore survive!

Procedure For Completing A Cashflow Forecast

Complete the form as follows (in pencil to allow changes), omit the £ signs and exclude pence:

1. Working ACROSS the sheet, write in the months (top line).
2. Now for the first month, fill in the SALES (line 1), unless you are doing a "break-even" cashflow in which case this comes at the very end.
3. Miss out line 2 at this stage, but fill in lines 3, 4 and 5.
4. Fill in lines 6 to 28, missing out lines 8, 10, and 13 (also 25 if not VAT-reg'd).
5. Now take line 28 from line 5 to get line 29 and add lines 29 + 30 to get 31.
6. Repeat this for the whole year. You will almost certainly have a lot of negative figures in line 31 (if not, you do not need a loan and lines 2 and 13 will remain zero). Assuming your line 31 figures are negative, try to estimate how much money you need for capital expenditure (this would normally be funded by a loan, HP or lease) while stock/raw materials would normally be funded by an overdraft. The cashflow should indicate a diminishing overdraft requirement.
7. Put any loan requirement figure into line 2 and check the sum of that amount and the overdraft does not exceed your line 3 as, remember, banks prefer not to put more money than you do into a project. Now fill in lines 8 and 13.
8. Now you can see what drawings (line 10) the business can support.

Note: Doing Cashflow Forecasts by hand takes time and care. A small computer using a spreadsheet program can allow you to do it much more easily.

<u>Miss Joan Smith</u>

<u>T/A SIMPLY PERFECT</u>

<u>BUSINESS PLAN</u>

Home Address:

12, Glasgow Street
Greenock PA1 1ZZ
Tel: Greenock (01475) 323

Author's Note: Please remember this is a fictitious Business Plan included to illustrate how such a plan might be written and presented. Your own Business Plan should be written in your own words and should incorporate your own data and figures.

SUMMARY

Nature of Business : Retail shop (Ladies outerwear fashion for the over 50s)

Location : Greenock

Proprietor : Miss Joan Smith

Staff : Proprietor only

Market : The main market is ladies, over 50, living in Greenock (population: 66,500). The nearest shops catering specifically for this market are in Paisley, 18 miles distant.

Premises Required : About 500 sq ft in a good location

Proposed Shop Name : Simply Perfect

Turnover : First year estimate approx £34,500
Second year estimate approx £40,000

Financing : Depending upon which shop is rented, capital of approximately £10,500 is required of which the proprietor can raise £6,500 leaving a balance of £4,000 to be found. A 3-year bank loan of £2,000 would be sufficient with in addition an overdraft facility of £2,000 to allow for stock purchases in the initial months.

INTRODUCTION

The objective is to set up a ladies outerwear fashion shop in the town centre of Greenock. The purpose of this Plan is to raise the finance for the venture.

PERSONNEL

Management.   The shop will be under the direct supervision of the proprietor, Miss Joan Smith. After working as a primary school teacher, Miss Smith, age 42, has spent 7 years in the retail trade, initially as a shop assistant and more recently as Assistant Manageress of the Miss Jones boutique in Gourock. Miss Smith owns her own flat. She plans to attend evening courses on elementary book-keeping at the local College.

Staff.   Miss Smith does not plan to employ any staff. However her sister, who lives locally and has experience of working in shops, is able to assist her should the need arise.

SERVICE

Service Description.   The shop will stock ladies outerwear aimed mainly at the over 50s age group. Garments will include dresses, skirts, blouses, overcoats, raincoats, hosiery, hats and accessories and will be in styles and sizes appropriate to that age group.

Market Research & Marketing Plan.   Miss Smith has observed during her years in retail in the area that many of her older clientele complained that they were obliged to travel to Paisley, some 18 miles away, to find good clothes shops to suit them. This prompted Miss Smith to investigate the market further. The population of Greenock is 66,500 but it is a spread out town adjoining two other towns, Gourock to the west and Port Glasgow to the east, thus the potential market is larger than just that of Greenock itself. The existing shops in the area which might present competition to her venture are as follows:

Icebergs   —   A large Department store catering to a wide age group with a
                         limited range for the over 50s.

Inver-Fashions   —   A new upmarket shop but with relatively high prices and fashions
                         more appropriate to younger customers.

Miss Jones   —   A small boutique with only skirts and dresses for this age group.

At present therefore there is little direct competition from stores in Greenock or its neighbouring towns, Gourock and Port Glasgow. The main competition are the stores in Paisley which these ladies visit.

Miss Smith has questioned a sample of 50 ladies who she knows and who would all be potential customers of her new store. Of these 44 said they would at least consider a shop locally in preference to one 18 miles away in Paisley. The only reservations were expressed by 6 ladies whose work took them to Paisley anyway and so they would continue to visit the shops there.

To promote the shop the proprietor plans to organise fashion shows at the local Ladies Luncheon Club and the Tuesday Club. She will also advertise these special events in the local newspaper and monitor the response carefully. She would also change the shop window weekly as she believes that is an important way to promote her stock.

<u>Suppliers</u>. Miss Smith has attended two national fashion trade shows and has spoken to 15 potential suppliers who carry appropriate lines and they have almost all stated that they would normally offer 30 days credit on receipt of satisfactory references. This credit is not reflected in the Cashflow as the suppliers stated that this credit facility would only come into effect after an initial order or two had been placed and paid for satisfactorily.

PREMISES & EQUIPMENT

<u>Premises</u>. A shop to rent of around 500 sq ft is required sited preferably on West Street or Regent Crescent, possibly Hill Lane. These are near the town centre but do not attract the very high rents of Main Street. There are two vacant shops which may be suitable and the Cashflow Forecast reflects the rent and rates of the shop at 12 Regent Crescent. This shop is available on a 7 year lease (with rent and rates of £6,500 pa). Although this site is on the edge of the prime town centre shopping area, it is situated between the main car park and the town centre shops, so many people walk by.

<u>Equipment</u>. Certain equipment (some purchased second-hand) would be required. In addition the shop at 12 Regent Crescent would require its interior repainted, the exterior being satisfactory though a new shop sign would be required. The start-up capital expenditure costs are listed as an Appendix to this Business Plan.

<u>Transport</u>. The business does not require transport and so Miss Smith does not plan to purchase a vehicle. Stock ordered by her at trade shows or through suppliers Reps will be despatched to the shop by normal parcel delivery services.

LEGAL ASPECTS

The situation regarding Planning Permission has been investigated with the local authorities. Since the intention is to trade from premises which have recently been used for similar retailing purposes Miss Smith has been informed that no application for Planning Permission is required.

FINANCIAL

Pricing.   Garments and accessories in the shop will reflect the mark-ups typical of the fashion trade locally which are 80% to 120%.

Cashflow Forecast.   The attached Cashflow Forecast shows a turnover in the first year of £34,500 at which the business is just above break-even, but it is thought that by the second full year of operation the turnover will rise to around £40,000. The sales estimates are based on two different calculations which both arrive at a minimum turnover of around £35,000. In the first method Miss Smith has estimated her proposed shop's first year's sales to be 75% of that done by the boutique Miss Jones where she worked recently. Second, she has calculated the likely turnover in terms of the Rate of Stock Turn which is defined as the turnover divided by the stock value (at retail prices). Hence a stock value of £14,000* and a turnover of £35,000 would give a Rate of Stock Turn of 2.5 which should be obtainable.

It is also assumed that there will be Solicitor's fees of £300 for arranging the lease on the shop, insurance has been quoted at £350 and accountant's fees of £400 have been allowed for.

Project Risk Assessment.   It is Miss Smith's opinion that the local market can sustain another specialist shop in addition to her proposed venture so that should a second shop open at some future date her project would not be jeopardised. If sales were 20% less than forecast, the business would survive, albeit with difficulty. Finally, should Miss Smith take ill, her sister would run the shop.

Financial Requirements.   Depending upon which store is rented, approximately £10,500 capital is required of which the proprietor can raise £6,500. A 3-year bank loan of £2,000 would pay for setting up costs (mainly equipment), while an overdraft of £2,000 would assist with the provision of stock.

*Author's Note: In this example, £14,000 at retail prices is stock valued at around £7,000. You will notice from the worked example cashflow that in May the shop purchases £5,000 of stock. Over the next few months the stock level rises as monthly purchases exceed sales.

START-UP CAPITAL EXPENDITURE

Fixtures & Fittings

Shelving	£150.00
Display Units	£290.00
Exterior Shop Sign	£250.00
Repaint Shop Interior	£150.00
Additional Lighting	£100.00
Mirrors (for changing room)	£ 30.00
Curtains (for changing room)	£ 80.00

Equipment

2nd Hand Cash Till	£200.00
Pricing Gun	£ 50.00
2nd Hand Mannequin	£100.00
Clothes Hangers	£ 50.00
TOTAL:	£1450.00

PROJECTED PROFIT & LOSS ACCOUNT

SALES	£34,500 [1]
LESS COST OF SALES	£17,250 [2]
GROSS PROFIT	£17,250

LESS EXPENSES: [3]

Advertising & Promotion	£ 400
Bank Interest	£ 91
Business Insurance	£ 350
Electricity/Gas/Heat	£ 575
Fees	£ 700
Loan Interest	£ 269 [4]
Motor	£ 0
Postage/Carriage	£ 0
Rent & Rates	£6500
Repairs & Maintenance	£ 200
Staff Wages	£ 0
Stationery/Printing	£ 40
Sundries	£ 260
Telephone/Fax	£ 600
Travelling	£ 200
Depreciation: [5]	
Fixtures & Fittings	£ 262
Equipment	£ 100
	£10,547

NET PROFIT	£ 6,703 [6]

Author's Notes:
(1) If VAT-registered, Sales = Turnover (ie Total Sales) less VAT.
(2) In this case, this equals the value of stock sold which produced the £34,500 sales. Estimated here using an average mark-up of 100%. (To get this figure at year end, one would add up all stock purchased and deduct the value of stock in the shop after the last day of trading in the financial year).
(3) If VAT-registered, all these figures are less any VAT charged.
(4) Only the interest is tax deductible. Here the £2000 loan is repaid in 36 months at £80/month (obviously this rate can vary), so there is interest of:
$[(£80 \times 36) - £2000] \div 36 = £24.44$/month x 11 months this year.
(5) See note on depreciation on page 11.
(6) The Net Profit needs to equal or exceed the Proprietor's Drawings (allowing for National Insurance contributions and any Income Tax that may be due).
(General) Capital Expenditure, Proprietors Drawings and Vehicle Purchase costs would not appear on the P & L Account as they are not tax deductible items.
(General) This is a simplified P & L to illustrate the main features. For instance, it omits bank charges. In practice you also usually have "accruals". This is because your financial year will not coincide exactly with the periods for rent, rates, phone rental etc, but you must take these into account, as part of these liabilities relate to the financial year covered by the P & L.

CASHFLOW FORECAST

	CASH IN	MAY	JUN	JUL	AUG	SEP	OCT	NOV	DEC	JAN	FEB	MAR	APR	TOTALS
1	Sales (inc VAT)	1000	1500	2000	3000	3000	2750	4000	8000	1500	1750	2750	3250	34500
2	Bank or other Loans		2000											2000
3	Owner's Capital	6500												6500
4	Other Money In													
5	TOTAL	7500	3500	2000	3000	3000	2750	4000	8000	1500	1750	2750	3250	43000
	CASH OUT (inc VAT)													
6	Stock/Raw Materials	5000	3000	1500	1250	1500	1375	2000	4000	750	875	1375	1625	24250
7	Advertising & Promotion	200						200						400
8	Bank Charges/Interest			44			38			9				91
9	Business Insurance	350												350
10	Drawings/Salaries/NI		300	300	300	500	500	500	800	700	700	700	700	6000
11	Electric/Gas/Heat		75		75		75		125		125		100	575
12	Fees (eg Accountant, Lawyer)	300										400		700
13	HP/Lease/Loan Payments		80	80	80	80	80	80	80	80	80	80	80	880
14	Motor — Fuel													
15	— Other Expenses													
16	Postage/Carriage													
17	Rent & Rates	1000	250	250	1250	250	250	1250	250	250	1250	250		6500
18	Repairs & Maintenance		50			50			50			50		200
19	Staff Wages													
20	Staff PAYE/NI													
21	Stationery/Printing	20						20						40
22	Sundries	80	50	30	20	10	10	10	10	10	10	10	10	260
23	Telephone/Fax	250	50			100			100			100		600
24	Travelling					100							100	200
25	VAT													
26	Other Expenses													
27	CAPITAL EXPENDITURE	1450												1450
28	TOTAL	8650	3855	2204	2975	2590	2328	4060	5415	1799	3040	2565	3015	42496
29	Net Cashflow	(1150)	(355)	(204)	25	410	422	(60)	2585	(299)	(1290)	185	235	504
30	Opening Balance	0	(1150)	(1505)	(1709)	(1684)	(1274)	(852)	(912)	1673	1374	84	269	0
31	**CLOSING BALANCE**	(1150)	(1505)	(1709)	(1684)	(1274)	(852)	(912)	1673	1374	84	269	504	504

Author's Note: Figures in brackets are negative, ie the business bank account would be in overdraft.

Raising the Finance

HOW much money do you need for your new venture? Hopefully this question would have been answered while you were putting together the Business Plan. Basically what you need to know is how much money you will need for:

a) Start-Up Capital   This is the money for the one-off start-up costs such as buying machinery or vehicles, developing or launching a product, fitting out a shop, equipping an office etc.

b) Working Capital   This is the short-term borrowing requirement which is usually caused by the time delay between you buying something and reselling it (as in a shop) or the delay between providing a service and being paid for it or the delay between buying raw materials and selling the finished product.

The amount of money that you can raise has certain limits which are discussed in a moment. If you cannot raise the money that the Business Plan indicates is necessary, then you either have to scale down the project, change the concept or you may even have to abandon it altogether.

If you start on a small scale and your business is profitable then you should be able to attract increased finance for expansion at the appropriate time.

SOURCES OF FINANCE

To raise the money to start the business will almost certainly require funds from a number of sources.

In virtually every case, one or more of the Proprietors or Directors will have to put up a reasonable proportion of the funds required.

Your accountant or business adviser can suggest which banks and financiers you might approach.

The various sources of £ are as follows:

1. Yourself!
2. Friends and Relatives.
3. The Banks.
4. Government.
5. Equity Financiers *(for Ltd Co. only)*
6. HP/Leasing Firms.
7. Trade Credit.
8. Other Sources.

Each of these are now considered in turn . . .

1. YOURSELF

This is obviously the first place to look for money to start your own business. In addition to any spare cash you may have in the bank, building society or as shares you can also raise money by selling possessions.

"Luxury" possessions that could be sold to raise cash might include: stereos, photographic equipment, video cameras and recorders, colour TVs, jewellery, caravans, dinghies, furniture and so on. Setting up a business can involve considerable sacrifice and a drop in your living standards until the business is established.

Another possibility if you own a newish car is to sell it and buy a cheaper older one (or a van if that was better suited to the proposed venture), but obviously if your intended business involved a lot of driving then purchasing an old high-mileage vehicle may be unwise.

If larger sums of money are necessary you could consider selling your house (assuming you own it of course) and

buying a more modest home – though check first what the legal expenses might add up to as that may cancel out the gain. A better idea may be to have a second mortgage on your existing home. This is only possible if the property is worth considerably more than the existing mortgage, allowing scope for the second mortgage on the unmortgaged part of the house value. Note though that second mortgages tend to be expensive.

A final, cautionary point is if you need to borrow large sums of money, almost certainly you will be asked for personal guarantees, ie should the venture fail, you will be called upon to honour the debt which may bankrupt you or make you homeless!

KEY POINT Read the small print of any personal guarantee, get legal advice and consider this very carefully indeed.

Other points to note:

Situation: No Funds   If you have either no money or can only contribute a very small portion of the total required, then you may have difficulty in raising the balance simply because potential financial backers, such as banks, do not like to feel they are taking the lion's share of the risk. An alternative to money is capital you can introduce by way of machinery, plant, vehicles, equipment and even business premises, however modest.

Situation: Sufficient Funds In contrast to having no funds, if you have sufficient funds to finance the complete project yourself, you might not think of talking to your bank, accountant or any other financial specialist. In some ways this

DIFFERENT FINANCIAL PACKAGES

Unless you are funding the new project entirely yourself, there are a number of ways in which the necessary finance can be put together. The process usually becomes ever more complex as the sums of money increase. The diagrams below should give you an idea of the typical financial packages to raise capital from £1,000 up to £250,000 or more.

Case I

In the case of a very small project requiring, say under £2,000, and where the proprietor has no capital, a bank may be prepared to provide an overdraft, particularly if there is adequate security. Being on an Enterprise scheme with a guaranteed regular allowance might help encourage a bank to lend money.

O/DRAFT

Case II

This is a very typical situation, where the proprietor raises the start-up capital (possibly by borrowing from friends and relatives) and the bank provides an overdraft to meet the working capital requirements of the business.

YOUR CAPITAL   **O/DRAFT**

Case III

Where there is a grant available the maximum likely bank funding may be increased. (In this case as a bank loan).

BANK LOAN   **GRANTS**   **YOUR CAPITAL**   **O/DRAFT**

Case IV

This is another typical situation, where the proprietor puts up at least half the necessary money with the bank providing the rest, partly as a short-term loan and partly as an overdraft.

BANK LOAN   **YOUR CAPITAL**   **O/DRAFT**

Case V

In the case of a franchise, a bank may be prepared to lend up to 60% or even 70% of the capital requirements.

BANK LOAN   **YOUR CAPITAL**   **O/DRAFT**

Case VI

This package is for a limited company with an outside investor, possibly a venture capitalist if the project is in the £50,000 + league.

BANK LOAN   **INVESTOR**   **YOUR CAPITAL**   **O/DRAFT**

can be a disadvantage because you miss out on the considerable expertise of these people. Also, because you do not have to convince would-be lenders of the viability of your project you may not prepare as conscientious a Business Plan. You should always prepare such a Plan and ask your accountant to read it through and comment. Your bank will probably ask to see it when you approach them to open an account. If anyone expresses doubts, then you should take another very hard look at the venture and do not be so sure that it is going to work.

2. FRIENDS & RELATIVES

Many people shy away from this good source of money. Care is required to avoid family friction – select only those people who could afford to lose what you are asking, then show them your Business Plan, ask them for a specific amount and do mention that you do not expect an immediate reply as you would like them to think it over.

If your friends or relatives agree to help fund your business it is essential that whatever is agreed is put down in writing. Unless it is a very small loan, the document should be drafted by a solicitor and it should specify:

a) the amount of the loan,

b) when it is due,

c) when the loan is to be repaid (be realistic here),

d) how the loan is to be repaid if the business runs into trouble (usually the repayment period is extended),

e) what interest (if any) is to be paid,

f) to what extent the lender can interfere with the business,

g) who the money should be repaid to in the event of death of the lender

h) what should happen if the business ceases to trade.

In the case of a "sleeping partner" the loan conditions could be detailed in the Partnership Agreement, and in the case of shares in a limited company the Memorandum and Articles of Association could cover these conditions.

Friends and relatives can help fund your venture in any (or a combination) of the following ways:

Loan (Interest Free)   This is usually reserved for loans made by close family or possibly a very close friend. The loan would normally be repaid within months rather than years.

Loan (With Interest)   For situations other than that mentioned above it is more appropriate that interest is added. The simplest approach is to use a fixed rate of interest based on the average "bank base rate" taken over the previous 12 months (this is to avoid artificial peaks and troughs in the rate). Alternatively, you could use the bank base rate current during the period of the loan, which although more difficult to calculate, is a much fairer method as it takes into account fluctuations in bank interest rates.

Choosing the bank base rate is useful for it not only saves argument but it is also cheaper for the would-be borrower (as banks normally charge more than base rate) and it is also often a better rate of interest than the lender would get from simply putting the money in a bank or building society. Note you may get tax relief on the interest you have to pay.

"Sleeping Partner"   Whereas with a loan your friends or relatives would not normally have any "say" in the running of your business, in this case the money is invested as risk capital and although the lender may not do the

day-to-day work, he or she should certainly have a say in how the business is run. As a partner they should be aware of their liability for any debts the business may build up. As a "sleeping partner" they should not draw a wage for they are not doing the day-to-day work, instead they should take a proportion of the net profits of the business (ie the profit after all expenses and your agreed "wage" have been deducted) at the end of the financial year.

One suggestion for the division of profits is they could be in the same ratio as the capital originally invested in the business, ie if you put £3,000 into the business at the start and the "sleeping partner" puts in £5,000 then you could share the profits as $3/8$ to yourself and $5/8$ to your partner. In addition you should have a "wage".

For a Limited Company Only   In this case the lender could opt to invest in the business by buying shares (refer also to **5. EQUITY FINANCIERS** below). Note that in a limited company, he who has the majority shareholding can dictate how the company will be run! This is unlike a partnership where (unless the Partnership Agreement states to the contrary) the partners have an equal say in the running of the business even if their capital contributions vary.

3. THE BANKS

Banks are in the business of lending money so they are constantly on the look-out for good business propositions in which to invest. The so-called "High Street" Clearing Banks are these days much more interested in the small business sector. One must say, however, that new businesses present a considerable risk, so banks

Raising the Finance

are naturally cautious. They will want to know full details of the proposed business and the people behind the project. The Business Plan you will have prepared is precisely the document for that purpose.

In addition to reading the Business Plan the bank manager may be keen to meet not only the people behind the plan but also their spouses (partners) and accountants. For although a carefully prepared Business Plan is important, the banker knows that if things should go wrong then it will be the calibre of the people behind the project and the support they get that will count towards redeeming the project and preventing a complete failure.

Shared Risk   Banks prefer the risk of a new venture to be shared and rarely like to put up more than 50% of the capital. In the case of franchises, with any well-known franchise company, the banks are sometimes prepared to lend up to 60% or more of the total capital requirements, provided of course that the projected profits of the business can sustain the loan repayments. This generous attitude to selected franchises is simply because of their proven success rate, but it should be pointed out that taking on a franchise can be an expensive way to start in business.

Loans & Overdrafts

Loans   These are normally made to finance the purchase of the fixed assets of the business (ie plant, equipment and buildings). These loans can be at either fixed or variable rates of interest and are repaid either monthly or quarterly over a pre-agreed "term",

usually 2 to 5 or more years (often longer for buildings).

Overdrafts   In contrast, overdrafts are for short-term working capital. This can bridge the gap: a) between buying stock and reselling it; b) providing a service (particularly to trade customers) and waiting up to 30 days or much longer to be paid or c) buying raw materials and later selling a manufactured product.

An overdraft, if granted, will be for an agreed amount. *Never* exceed this limit without prior permission from the bank manager, because the facility can be withdrawn at any time if the bank thinks you are mishandling your financial affairs.

An overdraft is usually the cheapest money you can borrow for your business, as you only pay interest on the daily balance "in the red". This interest being deducted automatically from your business bank account, usually each quarter.

Many businesses require a combination of loan and overdraft facilities when they start up. All banks publish and display their "Base Lending Rate" – as a small business you will normally pay several % more for your loan or

overdraft. Ensure you know what rate you are going to be charged and remember it is negotiable!

The Small Firms Loan Guarantee Scheme   This is a scheme whereby the government takes some of the risk in backing small business by underwriting a proportion of the loan so the bank's risk is reduced. The scheme is intended for new or established small firms with a viable business proposition that have tried and failed to obtain a conventional loan, either due to a lack of security or business track record. It is not available for all types of business, eg retailing is excluded.

There is a small premium to pay but in practice the repayments can be similar to a normal business loan. For more information, contact your own bank.

Security   Although you should not start by offering security, a bank will normally request this to cover any loan should the business fail. In any event you should not agree to security in excess of the value of loan you are requesting. Types of security include:

a) Guarantors   This is where someone else with suitable personal or business assets guarantees to pay the bank should you default.

b) Your Home (if you own it!) Where the market value of the house, less the outstanding mortgage, is substantial in comparison to the size of loan requested, then a home can provide useful and non-onerous security. Where this is not the case then it is best not offered nor accepted for security due to the unnecessary additional strain on the entrepreneur and his or her family. The bank is able, and will, foreclose on the mortgage in the event of a business failing, no matter how small the amount owed, and the borrower will lose his or her home.

c) *Your Work Premises* In contrast, if you own your shop, office or workshop, this could be excellent security.

d) *Life Assurance Policies* This applies primarily to those policies with a surrender value.

e) *Life Insurance* Depending upon your age, the size of loan you require and what other security is offered, a bank may require a life insurance policy to be payable to the bank to cover its loan should you die prematurely.

f) *(For a Limited Company only)* There are two commonly used forms of security. The first is *Directors' personal guarantees* where the Directors pledge to pay up from their personal funds should the business be unable to make the loan repayments. This effectively removes one of the advantages of forming a company and the limited liability protection it offers. If personal guarantees are sought, read the small print carefully and take legal advice.

The second commonly used form of security is the *floating charge* where the bank has rights over the assets of a company as these change (ie float up and down) as, for instance, stock levels vary.

KEY POINT If a bank turns you down, ask them why? It may be the project is simply too risky and you would be wise to modify or abandon it.

Shopping Around Assuming your project is likely to be viable (and that is in other people's opinion too, not just your own) then if you do not get what you require from your own bank or the conditions they want to attach (such as personal guarantees) are unacceptable then it is worth shopping around.

4. GOVERNMENT

It makes good sense for anyone setting up in business to fully explore what government grants, "soft" loans, subsidies or other assistance is available, though it must be pointed out that for a significant majority of business start-ups there is little help available in terms of hard cash.

A Business Plan will almost always be required. It is advisable to approach the relevant agency before you actually commence trading or set up your business and your Business Plan should demonstrate a clear need for the assistance.

KEY POINT For more information, in England contact your local Business Link. In Scotland, contact your Business Shop. In Wales, contact your TEC and in N. Ireland, contact LEDU (Tel: 01232 491031).

What government help there is comes from many sources (the EC, Central and Local Government) and is channelled through many different bodies. It can also vary considerably from one area of the country to another, but as a general guide this usually provides help under the following broad categories:

Premises Some incentives relate to premises but these are mainly (not

... do not be too upset if there are no grants for your project!

exclusively) available for manufacturing businesses. Such incentives can include rent-free periods (which can be several months, possibly up to 2 years) or stepped rents, reduced rates, and sometimes grants towards paying for new buildings, extensions or renovation work.

Equipment Again, most incentives which relate to equipment are for manufacturing businesses.

Technology There might be some assistance for research and technology projects.

Training There are some schemes around to encourage the employment and training of staff. Where available, these usually subsidise the wages of a new employee (ie pay a portion of the

Raising the Finance

wage bill for a set time), provide a straight cash lump sum if one takes on staff or they pay wages during a set training period. There are also some special schemes to encourage the employment of long-term unemployed, people with disabilities and youngsters.

"Enterprise Allowance"

This was an excellent national scheme (also known as the EAS) to help unemployed people who were trying to set up in business for themselves. The scheme still exists but is now managed locally and is known by different names. It provides an allowance for unemployed people in the early stages of starting their own business.

Assisted Areas

There are several important Department of Trade and Industry grants available to businesses operating in the Assisted Areas (as shown on the map). For further information on these grants, in England contact your local Business Link, in Scotland contact the Scottish Office Industry Department at Meridian Court, 5 Cadogan Street, Glasgow G2 6AT, tel: 0141-248 4774.

5. EQUITY FINANCIERS

(This only applies if you plan to set up a Limited Company).

There are two very good reasons for having an outside investor in your business – first, they can contribute business knowledge or contacts and second, by having the money invested as equity (shares) rather than loans you do not become "over-geared". (*Note:* Over-gearing is where the ratio of loans to share capital is such that the business's profits cannot support the interest payments on the loans and thus the business slowly sinks).

□ Development Area

■ Intermediate Area

Assisted Areas

50

Since an investor should contribute their knowledge in addition to capital, choose these partners carefully and ask pointedly what they can offer by way of expertise, trade and customer contacts in addition to money.

Many people want to retain 100% control and ownership of their new business because they are convinced they will make their "millions" from it and they do not feel inclined to share the spoils. However, it takes a good deal of investment and business acumen to make one's fortune and those elusive millions are much more readily achievable if one is prepared to have a slice of a large cake rather than the whole of a small cake.

Equity finance can come from one or indeed a combination of two main sources:

Private Investors In this case an individual invests directly in the business by purchasing shares. Shares are often a nominal £1 and so if the total capital being invested was £10,000 you may be investing £6,000 of your own (you will thereby own 60% of the company) while the other shareholder(s) invest the remaining £4,000. Thus there will be £10,000 of "issued share capital". If you did not want to give up as much of the equity or you wanted more funds, then this could be in the form of loans or by setting up more complicated financial structures. Note that an investor is better protected if some of his (or her) money is in the form of a loan, for if the business fails he (or she) is more likely to get some of the loan money back, whereas the share capital is likely to be lost.

Venture Capitalists This is for projects which are on the larger side of "small" with start-up capital in the £50,000 + category. Venture capitalists split into

Would you share your cake?

two entirely different sets of organisations with different motives. On the one hand there are the government development agencies who sometimes take an equity share in a new company if they see it to be a desirable business while on the other hand there are the private sector venture capitalists who are looking for a healthy return on their investment.

Whereas the development agencies are prepared to make investments as low as £10,000, the private sector venture capitalists are not normally interested in investments below the £50,000 mark (indeed many have higher thresholds) though as usual there are exceptions.

The largest company of its type in the field is *3i* (formerly Investors In Industry) which was formed in 1945. They have offices in most major cities and their London office is at 91 Waterloo Road, London SE1 8XP, tel: 0171-928 3131.

The "High Street" banks may also provide equity finance for larger projects.

Note that you usually have to pay fees for acquiring venture capital money. You may be charged "negotiation fees" (also called "commitment fees") for arranging the finance. This can vary from 2% to 7% which together with legal fees can reach 10% of the sum raised. In addition, some organisations also charge annual "management" fees.

An attractive point of equity finance is that companies, if empowered by their Articles of Association, can buy back their own shares out of capital provided certain safeguards are met. This mechanism may attract an outside investor as they can make a capital gain and recover their investment (assuming the business is successful) by selling back their shares to the company at a profit.

6. HP/LEASING FIRMS
Generally this is a more expensive way of raising finance than using a bank. However it can be useful for acquiring high value items such as cars, vans or machinery if one has difficulty raising the required capital.

Since the finance company usually retains ownership of the vehicle or equipment, they may be prepared to offer the finance even when your bank borrowing is on its limits. Obviously there is no point in negotiating a finance deal if you think you may have difficulty in meeting the repayments.

There are tax differences between Hire Purchase (HP) and Leasing which will require an accountant's advice. In every case, get quotes from several HP or Leasing firms and read the small print carefully as their interest rates and conditions can vary markedly.

Raising the Finance

7. TRADE CREDIT

Another excellent source of finance is trade credit. This is where a supplier allows you time before you have to pay for the goods or services they have provided.

If you do your cashflow assuming no credit and then do the same cashflow assuming your suppliers give you 30 days credit you will be amazed how this can often improve your figures dramatically.

One snag is that a new business is often asked to pay up-front as it is an unknown credit risk, so if you can negotiate any credit period it will be a great help. Once you are trading, you may, by negotiation, stretch the normal 30 day period to 60 days or even longer. You should of course pay your bills by the agreed date. Failure to do so is not only poor business ethics but your supplier will note this and may either eventually remove your credit facility or simply be less accommodating on other matters.

Trade credit is also relevant if your customers are mainly trade as they will expect credit (even if you are a new business). Credit control is vital to your cashflow. Issue your Invoices promptly and send out Statements at the end of the month (many companies pay only on Statements rather than Invoices) and follow up with phone calls if the payment date is passed. A suggestion to encourage their prompt payment is for you to offer a discount (2.5% is a typical figure) for payment made within 30 days. One tip is to highlight (in colour) on your invoices the date when payment is due.

8. OTHER SOURCES

Some business development agencies and local Enterprise Agencies have

Venture Capitalists looking for . . .
. . . a healthy return . . .

small sums of money (ie usually under £5,000 per project) for certain categories of applicants or projects in their area of operation.

For those individuals or businesses that meet certain specific requirements, there are other very useful sources of start-up finance:

Prince's Youth Business Trust This scheme was the Prince of Wales own idea and he is its President. The Trust helps 18 to 30 year olds, who are unemployed, under-employed or of limited means, to set up and run their own businesses. The Prince's Youth Business Trust provides financial help (mainly by soft loans) for applicants who have a viable business idea, but have been unsuccessful in raising the finance elsewhere to start their own venture.

An important feature is that each business has their own adviser appointed to help them and this help is ongoing.

The scheme is national with regional offices (tel: 0800 842 842), with the headquarters at: 18 Park Square East, London NW1 4LH, tel: 0171-543 1234.

In Scotland, there is the Prince's Scottish Youth Business Trust (PSYBT) which has slightly different rules. Their office is in Glasgow, tel: 0141-248 4999.

Livewire Another initiative aimed at helping young people to start their own businesses, Livewire provides advice for people aged 16 to 25 and awards cash prizes by their "Business Start Up Awards".

Livewire also operate their "Business Growth Challenge" programme where young owner managers spend a series of free residential weekends being given high quality management training to encourage further growth of their businesses.

Contact Livewire at Hawthorn House, Forth Banks, Newcastle-upon-Tyne NE1 3SG. Tel: 0191-261 5584 or 0345 573252.

British Steel (Industry) Ltd This organisation helps businesses to start up, expand or relocate in 20 traditional steel areas around the country. They provide loans and/or share capital in amounts from £10,000 to £150,000. They can also provide work space for small businesses in some of the areas. Tel: 0114-2731612.

Enterprise Investment Scheme This scheme aims to encourage investment in unquoted limited companies that need to raise start-up or expansion finance. The scheme does this by providing tax incentives to appropriate investors.

Enterprise Zones The zones can be quite small – often a specific industrial estate. Enterprise Zones last only 10 years and most have come to the end of their time, though there are a few new ones being created (mainly in former coalfield areas). The advantages of the Enterprise Zones usually include exemption from business rates and 100% tax allowances for any capital expenditure on industrial and commercial buildings. Planning permission is also simplified and individual zones may have other incentives.

KEY POINT Borrowed money has to be repaid! Ensure your Cash-flow Forecast permits you to repay loans even if bank interest rates rise and your turnover drops.

KEY POINT Most new businesses start under-capitalised and this makes them vulnerable. It is therefore important that your Business Plan allows for contingencies. It is easier to raise money before a project commences than after several difficult months of trading have elapsed■

Finding Premises

Y OUR business will need premises even if it is just the front room of your home. The choice of premises is important and in certain cases such as a shop, restaurant or hotel, the decision can either make or break the business.

GENERAL POINTS

To Buy or Rent?   If you can afford it and if you are planning to remain at one location for several years it may be better to buy the property as it provides more security in the longer term. However, when you are starting a business, you probably do not want all your funds to be tied up in bricks and mortar, and so you will have little option but to rent. One exception is if you are taking over a small hotel or guest house, it is more usual to *buy*.

Location   Many people look for premises near to where they live. That could lead to them setting up in either a poor location or at best a marginal location. It is better to ask yourself "Where is the best place to set up my business?" The answer may be in an adjacent town or county!

Planning Permission   Check with the Planning Department of the local Council that the existing planning permission for the premises you are considering covers the activities you plan to perform. If not, you will need to apply for a "change of use". This can take a month or more. Classes of use include: residential, retail (several classes), offices, light industrial etc. One situation where planning permission can be a problem is if you want to sell directly to the public from a small factory as that is usually classed as "mixed use" (retail and industrial) and may not be acceptable to the local Council. Planning Permission will also be required for proposed extensions, changes to frontages and external signs or advertisements. If any structural alterations are required this will also need formal approval.

Locating Premises   There is rarely one organisation that knows all the commercial properties to buy or rent in their area so you should do all of the following: a) contact your local Enterprise Agency or business development unit (especially for workshop and factory space), b) read the commercial property adverts in the local newspaper and c) visit estate agents who specialise in commercial property. You could also insert an advert in the local newspaper under the "Premises Wanted" classification.

In the case of retail premises you should also walk the shopping streets looking for "To Let" signs. Your Enterprise Agency or business development unit will be able to quote typical rental figures (which are usually given in terms of £ per square foot per year) and typical rates payable.

Always examine as many premises as possible to get the best property available. Don't just go for the first you see.

Fire Safety   If you employ anyone, you need to: a) ensure they have a means of escape in the event of fire, and b) provide a means of fighting a fire (eg a suitable fire extinguisher). If you employ 20 or more people (10 or more if they work above or below ground level) then you will need a Fire Certificate. Contact your local Fire Safety Officer.

The Lease   If renting, this is the lengthy and detailed tenancy contract. It is a very important document so read it carefully. It will cover – the period of lease, rent, all responsibilities including those for insuring and repairing the premises (normally the tenant's responsibility), statutory liabilities, when rent reviews are due and the use and transferability of the lease (you want to be free to pass on the lease). Note that many leases permit the landlord to raise the rent by a fixed amount whenever a lease is reassigned. If the lease states you are responsible for the dilapidations, ie deterioration of the building during your tenancy, you should get a survey done and agreed with the landlord (it is also a good idea to take some photos!). Leases are not set in stone, so challenge hostile or unreasonable clauses and question any you do not understand. Find out if there is a Factor who is managing the property and what his charges are and if there are common charges.

Surveyors   When you begin your search for premises another door you should knock on is that of a local chartered surveyor. He will advise you on suitable areas to look for premises, other areas to avoid, typical rents and so on. Once you have located premises (either to rent or buy) you would be advised to have the premises surveyed.

KEY POINT   *Never sign a lease* until you have completed your Business Plan, raised the finance, had the building surveyed and have discussed the lease terms in detail with your own solicitor.

KEY POINT   When you take over premises, remember to inform the local Authority (for Rates), BT, the P.O., the Factor (if any), and get the gas or electricity meters read the day you move in.

SHOP PREMISES CHECKLIST ✓

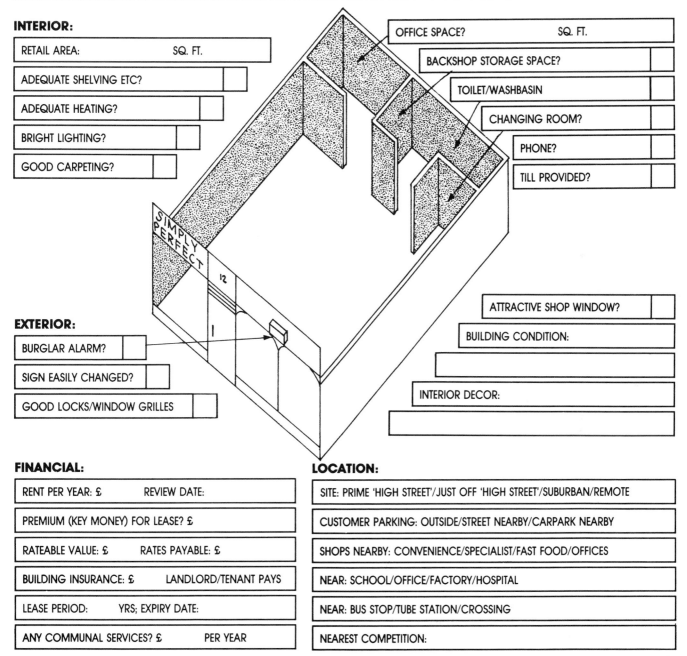

INTERIOR:

RETAIL AREA: SQ. FT.

ADEQUATE SHELVING ETC?

ADEQUATE HEATING?

BRIGHT LIGHTING?

GOOD CARPETING?

OFFICE SPACE?   SQ. FT.

BACKSHOP STORAGE SPACE?

TOILET/WASHBASIN

CHANGING ROOM?

PHONE?

TILL PROVIDED?

EXTERIOR:

BURGLAR ALARM?

SIGN EASILY CHANGED?

GOOD LOCKS/WINDOW GRILLES

ATTRACTIVE SHOP WINDOW?

BUILDING CONDITION:

INTERIOR DECOR:

FINANCIAL:

RENT PER YEAR: £   REVIEW DATE:

PREMIUM (KEY MONEY) FOR LEASE? £

RATEABLE VALUE: £   RATES PAYABLE: £

BUILDING INSURANCE: £   LANDLORD/TENANT PAYS

LEASE PERIOD: YRS; EXPIRY DATE:

ANY COMMUNAL SERVICES? £   PER YEAR

LOCATION:

SITE: PRIME 'HIGH STREET'/JUST OFF 'HIGH STREET'/SUBURBAN/REMOTE

CUSTOMER PARKING: OUTSIDE/STREET NEARBY/CARPARK NEARBY

SHOPS NEARBY: CONVENIENCE/SPECIALIST/FAST FOOD/OFFICES

NEAR: SCHOOL/OFFICE/FACTORY/HOSPITAL

NEAR: BUS STOP/TUBE STATION/CROSSING

NEAREST COMPETITION:

Finding Premises

DIFFERENT TYPES OF PREMISES

Working From Home   This is obviously the cheapest and simplest way for many businesses to start, and it is becoming popular, but there are legal constraints. In particular, if you live in a privately rented or council-owned house it will almost certainly be a breach of your tenancy agreement to conduct any business from your home. If you are a council tenant, a few discreet enquiries at the local government offices would let you know where you stand. Even if you own your home it may be an infringement of local planning regulations or bylaws to work from home and may also breach a condition of your ownership of the house. If you have a mortgage, the mortgage lender may not like it either. And if your neighbours object to your business activities, you could have a problem. So it is essential to get proper legal advice. In addition, ask your accountant about Capital Gains Tax and possible Business Rates implications.

Despite these hurdles, many businesses operate quite happily from homes (or domestic garages). They maintain a very low profile, with minimal advertising (or only using a telephone number on adverts), no exterior signs, no noise and no queues of visiting customers or suppliers . . . .

If you are thinking of working from home, you should always let your insurers know exactly what you are doing. There are now special policies for home-based businesses.

Many businesses operate happily from home . . .
. . . . maintaining a very low profile.

FURTHER READING   The whole subject of working from home is covered in depth in the companion book, ***The Greatest Guide to Home-based Business*** (see the end of this book for details).

Office   The main question to answer in this context is "Will customers need to visit the office and do they need to be suitably impressed?" If the answer is "no", you could opt for modest premises. If people are expected to visit you is there adequate car parking and is there public transport nearby? Be wary of upper floor offices with no lifts.

There are now office complexes where secretarial support (typing, reception, phone answering, fax, photocopying) is provided and this can be of great benefit to a small business not wanting to take on staff right away. In any office block be careful of your responsibilities for "common" repairs and any "joint management" charges for security, cleaning etc – all of which can be expensive. Finding suitable small office premises can be difficult. If the bulk of your work relates to one large company they may be happy to rent you a room in their own office block.

Shop   The 3 most important factors to consider when finding retail premises are: 1. Location, 2. Location and 3. Location! Remember too that the retail trade is changing – the chain stores have great financial and marketing strength; new shopping complexes are shifting the retail "centres" of towns, sometimes out of the town centres altogether; offices are encroaching on previously exclusive retail sites and shopping is becoming more of a family leisure activity. A street that was good for shopping in your childhood may now be a poor bet.

To assess a site, talk to people in the trade, talk to other shopkeepers nearby, take the advice of a local accountant and a local chartered surveyor. Visit the site at different times and different days of the week and count the passers-by. Are they carrying shopping? Are they to be seen in the shops or just walking past? Check too that there is suitable parking and access so stock can be delivered easily. But most important of all, be careful not to be taken in by the cheery facade and glitter of retail sites.

WORKSHOP/SMALL FACTORY CHECKLIST ☑

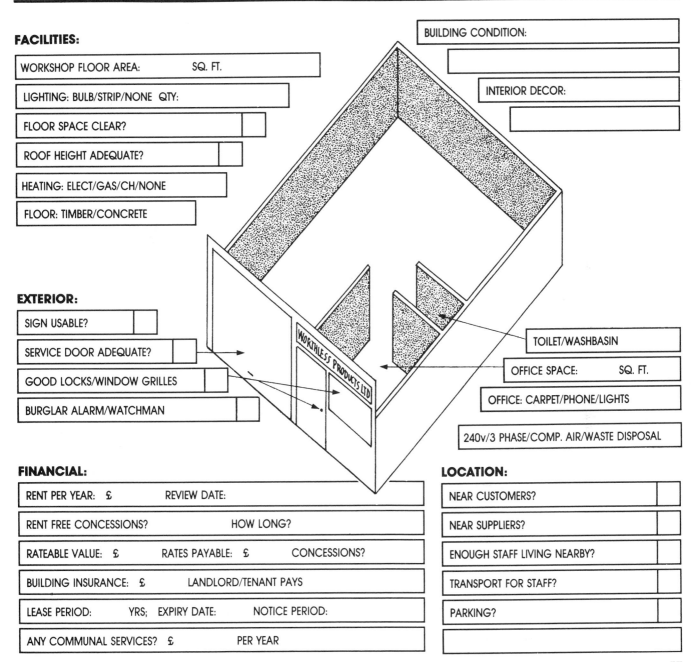

FACILITIES:

WORKSHOP FLOOR AREA: SQ. FT.

LIGHTING: BULB/STRIP/NONE QTY:

FLOOR SPACE CLEAR?

ROOF HEIGHT ADEQUATE?

HEATING: ELECT/GAS/CH/NONE

FLOOR: TIMBER/CONCRETE

EXTERIOR:

SIGN USABLE?

SERVICE DOOR ADEQUATE?

GOOD LOCKS/WINDOW GRILLES

BURGLAR ALARM/WATCHMAN

FINANCIAL:

RENT PER YEAR: £   REVIEW DATE:

RENT FREE CONCESSIONS?   HOW LONG?

RATEABLE VALUE: £   RATES PAYABLE: £   CONCESSIONS?

BUILDING INSURANCE: £   LANDLORD/TENANT PAYS

LEASE PERIOD: YRS; EXPIRY DATE: NOTICE PERIOD:

ANY COMMUNAL SERVICES? £   PER YEAR

BUILDING CONDITION:

INTERIOR DECOR:

TOILET/WASHBASIN

OFFICE SPACE: SQ. FT.

OFFICE: CARPET/PHONE/LIGHTS

240v/3 PHASE/COMP. AIR/WASTE DISPOSAL

LOCATION:

NEAR CUSTOMERS?

NEAR SUPPLIERS?

ENOUGH STAFF LIVING NEARBY?

TRANSPORT FOR STAFF?

PARKING?

WORTHLESS PRODUCTS LTD

Finding Premises

Check too with an insurance broker as certain areas (and certain types of stock) may be regarded as high risk from a security point-of-view and this could make your contents insurance expensive. The insurance companies might also insist on a burglar alarm which is an additional expense.

The demand for good shop sites is such that you may have to pay a "premium" (also called "key money") for the benefit of taking over a lease. This is a once-off payment for the privilege of taking over a desirable lease and it can be expensive. If the rent was set several years before and the next rent review is not due for a couple of years, then the incoming tenant *may* get the lease at the existing rent which could be lower than the going market rate. In that case, this benefit to the incoming tenant is often reflected in the premium he has to pay.

If your proposed shop is to stock food consult the Environmental Health Department of your local authority to ascertain what regulations are in force. Converting non-food premises for food may be very costly.. The choice of location for a shop is closely related to your market research results – see the chapter **Doing The Market Research**. See also the Checklist on page 55.

Workshop/Small Factory   There are new, old and refurbished units available almost everywhere but in certain areas of the country there will be a shortage of the most popular units (ie under 1,000 square feet). There are both private sector and government landlords (either local councils or development agencies). You *may* be able to extract more concessions from the latter but do not expect to pay much less than the privately owned units. The golden rule is to take on the smallest premises you can get by with but ensure your lease allows you to transfer to a larger unit, if required, without attracting financial penalties. Older premises tend to be cheaper though rents fluctuate widely depending upon the type of building and size, but can be higher for small custom-built "nursery" units.

If you are hoping to sell direct to the public from the unit or work on cars you may face problems with planning permission. In contrast, manufacturing businesses are considered particularly desirable by the government development agencies and various concessions may be negotiated such as rent free periods, reduced rates and so on. Remember that such "carrots" end so allow for this in your forward cashflow projections. Remember also to contact your local Health & Safety Executive officer (see the Phone Book) to find out what regulations are relevant to your proposed business. See also the Checklist on page 57.

Café/Restaurant/Bar   As with shops, location is crucial. Whereas a "fast-food" outlet or café requires a prime high street location a good restaurant or bar can afford to be elsewhere, but not just anywhere! Depending upon the clientele parking could also be essential. Check with the local Environmental Health Department for information on regulations and check too with the Fire Officer. If you plan to sell alcohol check on local licensing laws and opening hours. If the premises are not currently used for the same purpose then Planning Permission may be a problem.

Small Hotel/Guest House   To find the correct location for a hotel one must know *precisely* the clientele who would use the hotel. For instance, if it is mainly overnight Bed & Breakfast people then one needs to be in a highly visible location on a road carrying suitable traffic. In contrast, if it is mainly longer-stay tourists, one needs to be located where tourists go – contact your local Tourist Board to find out who comes, from where, at what times of the year, what accommodation they look for and whether the total numbers are rising or falling. If the clientele are mainly business people what accommodation do they require?

Before you either take over an existing hotel or convert a building to a hotel a great deal of market research must be done as once you buy you are heavily committed. Beware of buildings of "special architectural merit" especially if they are termed "listed buildings" as insurance cover could be extremely high and general repair work can be equally costly as it may be necessary to reinstate, for instance, ornate stonework.

If you own your own home you may consider selling it and putting the money towards the purchase of the hotel.

If you are going to serve food, you must contact your local Environmental Health Department at a very early stage as there are stringent regulations.

Note that if the hotel sleeps more than 6 people (including staff or guests) or if some sleeping accommodation is on any floor above the first floor or in the basement then it must have a Fire Certificate. You should also check on other local licensing requirements.

Adverts and estate agents are the best sources to find places to buy, and always have a full structural survey carried out before signing anything■

STARTING

Chapters

Designing Letterheads Etc

THE design of letterheads and business cards are not normally given enough consideration. They are a useful advert for your firm. When you send a letter to a prospective customer, it creates an instant impression of your business standards in terms of quality, professionalism and style. Often your letter will be you introducing your service to a new customer or it may be a quotation for a contract. In both cases you are trying to sell your business on the strength of what is on that small piece of paper – so it really is quite important.

Some business stationery uses striking colours, some use interesting artistic effects or graphic designs but even if yours is quite simple and produced on a low budget it is important that it is well laid out and smart. You will probably need the help of a professional designer or printer who will know how to get the best effect from a one colour print, an imaginative layout and well-considered choice of lettering.

Before doing anything some decisions have to be made:

Business Name In the chapter **Making It Legal** mention was made of trading under a business name rather than your own name. There are certain firms, such as solicitors, accountants and consultants, who traditionally trade under the names of the partners. Otherwise the opportunity of trading under a business name should not be missed. A business name should convey a sales message to your customers and is therefore a cheap yet powerful promotional tool. Some hints for choosing a business name are:

1. Pretend you are standing in your customer's shoes. What is it about your business that makes him or her choose *you?* Is it your speed, good service, wide choice of products, convenience, specialised service ... whatever it is, your name should reflect it.

2. Keep the name short. The "London Stainless Steel Flanged Bolts Co Ltd" may be a highly descriptive title but is obviously too long and will pose a problem should they diversify into brass!

3. Choose a word or words which roll off the tongue and are easy to say.

4. Check your local Phone Book to ensure no-one else has a similar business name. (If you are forming a limited company the company registration agent must check to ensure your proposed name is unique).

Company Logo A logo is a symbol by which you hope customers will identify you and your products. We are all familiar with logos and it can be an important promotional tool but it takes a long time and plenty of promotion before people learn to recognise it. Because of this it is not so useful when starting a small business, but if you have a good idea for a logo use it if you can.

Corporate Image Related to logos but of more relevance to a small company is to have a standardised corporate image. By this we mean standardised colour(s), graphics and typefaces which you use on everything related to the business – letterheads, business cards, invoices, products, packaging, promotional literature, advertisements, van sides, interior decor and even staff uniforms.

DESIGN ASPECTS

Colour Your business may be associated with something that people naturally identify with a given colour. Examples are: agriculture (green); aircraft/airlines (sky blue); shipping/marine (navy blue or grey); military (drab olive); sunshine (yellow) and so on. The primary colours (red, blue, yellow) tend to be associated with bold things, probably with a young image. In contrast, two-tone dark/light grey and brown/cream are more sophisticated. Gold and silver have appropriate connotations of wealth. Maroon, damson and violet are rich, possibly evening-related colours.

Before you get carried away remember that with anything you print each colour almost doubles the price and black printing is cheaper than any other colour. Remember too that if you choose a light colour (especially light blue) you will have difficulty making photocopies, if that is relevant.

Typefaces The different styles of lettering are known as typefaces and there are literally hundreds to choose from! Some commonly used typefaces are Univers, Helvetica (which is not unlike Univers) and Times Roman. These are also usually available in **bold** or *italic* forms. All lettering can be printed in different sizes, called the "point size". This book is set in 10 point, while this text is in 9 point and this text is in 11 point. A typeface just like a business name or colour conveys a message to the reader. For instance, the typeface called **STENCIL** looks rather military or related to packing cases (maybe an import/export business); an elaborate typeface such as *Script* looks rather dignified while 𝕺𝖑𝖉 𝕰𝖓𝖌𝖑𝖎𝖘𝖍 speaks for itself.

SIMPLY PERFECT

12 Regent Crescent
Greenock
PA1 1ZZ

Tel: Greenock (01475) 242

The shop for ladies who dress to perfection
Proprietor: Joan Smith

The Quick Guide to Letterheads

For a **Sole Trader** or **Partnership**, the example (left) shows the three legal requirements for a letterhead: a) business name, b) the name of the sole trader (or partners) and c) for each person named an address at which "documents can be served". Optional features shown here: a sales message, envelope fold line (on the left hand edge) and dots to place an address when using window envelopes.

Worthless Products Ltd

Unit 3
Industrial Estate
Birmingham B1 1ZZ

Tel: 0121-123 456
Fax: 0121-123 789

Manufacturers of Novelty Goods

Registered in England and Wales Registration Number: 00000
Registered Office: Unit 3, Industrial Estate, Birmingham B1 1ZZ

For a **Limited Company**, the example (right) shows the four legal requirements for a letterhead: a) full company name with Limited or Ltd, b) country of registration, c) registered number and d) the registered office address. Note that if you choose to add the Directors' names, then all names must be given.

(Note: These are both fictitious businesses).

Due to space limitations, we have not tried to show a clever design of letterhead or the use of logos etc.

DESIGNING A LETTERHEAD

This is assuming of course that your business venture actually needs a letterhead, if not, ignore this section.

Designing the letterhead involves choosing:

Paper Size   A4 (210 x 297mm) is very much standard in the UK. It fits most envelopes, files and photocopiers.

Paper Type   Letterheads are usually done on white paper. Coloured paper can be effective but has several disadvantages – it needs matching envelopes and second sheets, may photocopy poorly and it could be difficult to correct typing errors. The weight of paper is usually 75 or 100 grams/square metre but if you really want to impress, you can use the more expensive cartridge paper.

Typeface (ie Lettering)   See page 61. You may choose a fancy typeface for the business name and a plainer typeface, such as Univers, for the address.

Colour   Black is the cheapest colour to use for printing. All other standard colours are about the same price. Printing in two colours (black is also a "colour"), costs nearly double. With a single colour, additional effects can be achieved by using reverse text or "screening" which gives a lighter shade of colour. If you are trying to project a young and trendy image, gaudy colours may be fine, but remember that they might be inappropriate for, say, a sober engineering company.

Phone/Fax Details   An increasing amount of business is done over the phone. Here are several suggestions for a letterhead: a) if the number consists of a town name followed by the number, eg Oxford 123, then include the dialling code in brackets, eg Oxford (01865) 123, b) if you have a telephone answering machine connected it may be useful to note this because it warns the caller that they may find themselves speaking to a machine and it also indicates that a message can be left at any time and c) you may consider giving a home phone number in addition to an office number if you expect important calls outwith normal office hours. If you have a fax or telex machine then you should also print those numbers on the letterhead.

Sales Message   Your letter may be going to potential customers and it is therefore an excellent medium to carry a short sales message. Typical messages could be: a) names of companies you represent officially (if likely to be known to the reader), written along the top or bottom of the letterhead, b) the products or services your company provides or c) a message such as *"We import the finest silks"* or *"Manufacturers of Novelty Goods"* or whatever!

Other Information   Pre-printed words such as "Date: . . . Your Ref: . . .   Our Ref: . . .   File Ref: . . ." are becoming less fashionable and should only be added if you feel your own administration needs it.

Some Letterhead Legalities

For a sole trader or partnership the letterhead must, by law, include the following information: a) the business name (if one is used), b) the name of the sole trader (or the names of *all* partners) and c) for each person named, an address at which "documents can be served" (which in practice is often the business address).

For a limited company, the letterhead must, by law, include the following information: a) the full company name (including "Ltd" or "Limited"), b) the country of registration, c) the registered number and d) its registered office address (which may be different to the normal business address). If the letterhead is to show the Directors' names then every Director's name must be shown.

Layout

There are many acceptable styles of layout, but here are some tips:

1. Don't use print that is too small to read easily or a layout that forces the reader to search for your name, phone number etc.

2. Put the business name at the top, either centrally or to one side. Make it reasonably prominent.

3. Place the address block in the top right corner or perhaps along the foot of the letterhead.

4. Put Proprietor(s) names under the business name or at the foot of the letter.

5. Most envelopes require an A4 letterhead to be folded in three – a small printed "fold" line (about 5mm long) at the appropriate place on the left edge of the paper can make folding easier.

6. If you use "window" envelopes, mark the window area on the letterhead with tiny corner dots – this helps the typist. (Note: window envelopes save lots of time).

Designing Letterheads Etc

DESIGNING A BUSINESS CARD

A business card is useful whenever your business is such that you would normally know the name of your customer and he or she would know your name. It is therefore a very personal communication. It is almost essential if you are dealing with trade customers or government agencies. First, some basic design decisions need to be made:

Card Size   Many business people "file" the cards they receive in wallets or holders specially designed for the purpose. It is sensible therefore to keep your card to the standard size (ie about 9 x 5½cm) so that it will fit these holders. Another point is that business cards that open like greetings cards may not fit into these wallets or holders mentioned above.

Card Type   A thin floppy business card feels cheap and conveys a poor image.

Typeface And Colour   These should mimic the letterhead to get a standardised "corporate image".

Layout   There is much more freedom here than with a letterhead and scope for some interesting graphic design work. The most important aspect is to keep the name and job title clear and prominent. If more than one person in your business needs a business card, each card should be identical except for changing the name and job title.

The Information to be Printed on the Card

A business card carries different information to a letterhead for whereas a letterhead is issued by the *firm*, the business card is issued by an *individual* of that firm. So pride of place on the card should be given to the card user's name and position in the firm (ie your job title).

Name   Following American practice the business world seems to be dropping "Mr, Mrs, Miss or Ms" and using first names more. If you are selling *expertise* you could include any qualifications you have after your name.

Job Title   Your title is important as it conveys your status and area of responsibility. If there are two partners you could say "Partner" but it would be better to reflect the role they play, eg "Sales Manager" and for a limited company: "Sales Director", "Production Director" etc.

Firm's Name & Address   This should be complete with post code and phone/fax numbers. If dealing with overseas companies, do include "United Kingdom".

Sales Message   If space permits it is useful to put a sales message on your card, even if this is merely a brief statement as to what your firm does. Sales leaflets and brochures get misplaced and lost but people tend to hold on to business cards. If you are offering a service that a client will only require on occasions it is particularly important to word the message carefully as it could close a sale.

Reverse Side   Some people use this for their home address and phone number or a more extended sales message. It will cost more to print on both sides of the card and remember that in many business card wallets the reverse side gets covered by another card. Also, leaving the reverse blank can be useful for handwritten notes, off-the-cuff quotations etc.

OTHER STATIONERY

To save on printing costs for invoices, receipts and statements you can use a letterhead with the appropriate word, eg "INVOICE", typed as a heading (this practice is useful where the sums of money are large and you are not raising such invoices frequently). An alternative is to buy a rubber stamp (or small pre-printed labels) with your name and address (and VAT number if registered) and use one of the pre-printed duplicate books which are available from most stationers ■

ALMOST all businesses need to employ staff as they grow. Some of these people are excellent, but do think very hard before you take on any staff.

Employing anyone is very expensive – in addition to paying their wages when they are working, you have to pay them when they are on holiday or sick for a day or when they need an afternoon off to visit the dentist, and so on. Also, there is a tax on employment – it is called the Employers National Insurance contribution and it currently stands at 10% of wages for all higher paid staff. Finally, the paperwork and mandatory returns associated with employing staff is onerous and to cap it all staff can let you down badly. Keep in mind the golden rules:

● *Take on staff only if you have to.*

● *Beware of recruiting in anticipation of demand.*

● *Interview carefully.*

● *Get rid of bad employees as fast as legally possible.*

● *Encourage, train, reward and keep good employees.*

WHY EMPLOY STAFF?

Perhaps you do not need to actually employ staff at all or at least not yet. Here are some typical situations and possible solutions that save you from taking on more staff:

1. Telephone Answering You may think you need someone to answer the phone but an answering machine may be all you require or (in most cities) there are agencies that will take your calls for you for a fee. Or you could use a mobile phone if you are out and about a lot.

Perhaps you need some help?

2. Typing Letters You may be unable to type, but you may have a friend or relative who is prepared to type the odd letter for a nominal fee.

3. Office Work You may have a rush of office work – so why not use a "temp" from a secretarial agency?

4. Book-keeping All businesses need someone to keep the accounts books and if you do not want to yourself, then there are freelance book-keepers who will do the books for you.

5. Deliveries You may need someone to drive a van to deliver your products or collect materials, so why not use one of the many parcel services?

6. Selling You may need someone to go out and get orders. There are now organisations that specialise in

marketing other people's products and services. Alternatively you could use an agent (on commission) – but if you are thinking of this, take advice for it can be frustrating and unrewarding.

7. Manufacturing/Assembly Why not consider sub-contracting out your manufacturing or assembly work? This can apply to heavy, light or electronics engineering. Another way of sub-contracting is to use "cottage workers" (also called "outworkers") – this is where people work at home as if self-employed and it is used particularly for knitwear, garments and for "stuffing" electronic printed circuit boards. But a note of caution: many "outworkers" are now deemed to be employees under employment law, so first take advice.

RECRUITING STAFF

Before you start recruiting, you should draw up a *Job Description*, ie you need to be clear as to what you want the person to do. Also, decide if a part-timer might be sufficient to begin with.

Remember that you must not treat any job applicant less favourably on grounds of sex, race, colour, nationality, ethnic or national origin or on the grounds of disability.

There are several ways to find staff:

1. Card In Window For some low qualification jobs, you might advertise by putting a postcard in the window of the local newsagent.

2. Jobcentre These can be very useful and may, if required, do initial interviewing for you.

3. Newspaper Adverts This is obviously more expensive but casts your net wider. Choose a newspaper that your potential applicant is likely to read. For specialised jobs an advert in a trade or professional magazine may be more appropriate. Before you advertise, check several copies of the publication to see if there are similar adverts from other firms and what wages they are offering.

Your advert should describe the job adequately giving the wage offered and the likely age band and experience or qualifications of the applicant you are seeking. Try not to use a Box Number as this can be off-putting. Be careful about what you say – it must not be discriminatory and note that your advert may be contractually binding. Also, do not use the phrase "permanent employment".

4. Recruitment Agencies   These are expensive as they charge for the adverts they place plus a fee equivalent to 10% (or more) of the annual salary of the recruit. The main advantages of using an agency are they often have a number of suitable people on their books and they will do the initial interviewing of applicants.

Application Form   When applicants contact you, either send them or give them an Application Form to complete. See the example opposite. (To save space, the form has been condensed in size to one page – normally it would require two A4 sheets).

It is a good idea for Application Forms to be completed in hand-writing to see if the applicant's writing is decipherable. It may also reveal the attention to detail and care of the applicant – a messy Application Form is likely to come from a messy person!

Application Forms of unsuccessful candidates should be kept for 6 months or more in case of any complaints of racial/sexual discrimination. For any

candidate you take on you should keep the forms until some time after they leave your employment.

INTERVIEWING

An interview has two objectives – it allows the applicant to assess your firm and it allows you to assess the applicant. You need somewhere comfortable and quiet to conduct the interview, eg your business premises at the end of the working day (to prevent interruptions) or, you could use a "private function" room at a nearby hotel.

Make certain the applicants know where and when the interview is to take place. If you are interviewing several people one after another you need a second person (eg the Receptionist if using a hotel) to handle the new arrivals, and a separate waiting room for them. Allow at least an hour for each interview – much longer for key managerial jobs.

A common error when interviewing is our natural instinct to size up people in an instant by their physical attractiveness, dress and manner of speech. Try hard not to form an opinion until the end of the interview!

There is also the risk that candidates with physical characteristics or interests similar to the interviewer will be looked on too favourably.

Remember that not only is the applicant trying to "sell" himself or herself to your firm, but you also need to "sell" your firm as it is important to attract a good applicant to join.

Warning: A contract need not be in writing so if you make verbal promises during the interview they could be legally binding.

Competence Tests   It is always very important to check the skills of applicants. They may claim lots of

qualifications and/or experience but a few simple tests can prove revealing. For instance, if interviewing a potential secretary, ask them to type a letter and take dictation. Or when interviewing junior electronics technicians you could start by asking each of them to identify components on a printed circuit board and then ask them the function of these components. For a manual skill such as metalwork, joinery, welding etc set practical tests. In all cases these competence tests should be similar to the work the applicants would have to do in the job.

Where the competence being tested is more intellectual than manual, then another technique is to get the applicant to join you for a day when you are doing what the applicant would have to do if he or she got the job. For instance if you were recruiting a Sales Manager then by visiting customers with the applicant

---

SOME INTERVIEW TIPS . . .

Do put the applicant at ease
Do offer them a tea or coffee
Do sit at a similar height
Do get the applicant talking
Do ask open-ended questions
Do take notes

Don't have any interruptions
Don't be influenced by first impressions
Don't sit behind a desk
Don't sit with a bright light behind you
Don't avoid awkward questions
Don't forget to cover pay, holidays etc
Don't ask questions which may be considered discriminatory

STAFF APPLICATION FORM

Please answer ALL questions in INK, in your own hand-writing. Where there is an asterisk (*), please delete as necessary.

Position Applied For: . . . .

Full Name: Mr/Mrs/Miss/Ms* . . . . Single/Married/Divorced/Separated*

Date of Birth: . . . .

Present Address: . . . .

Tel No (Daytime): . . . .   Tel No (Evening): . . . .

No. and ages of dependent children: . . . .

National Insurance No: . . . .   UK Driving Licence No: . . . .

Details of any serious accidents/illnesses: . . . .

Educational Qualifications: *(box needs to be extended to provide space for answers)*

Dates		Names of all secondary schools, colleges and universities attended	For schools: exams passed and grades For higher educn: course and qualification
From	To		

Membership of any professional organisation: . . . .   Foreign languages: . . . .

Work Experience (including temporary and part-time): *(box needs to be extended to provide space for answers)*

Dates		Name and address of employer	Position held with details of duties	Salary on leaving £	Reason for leaving
From	To				

General:

What notice is required by your present employer: . . . . (Note: We will not contact your present employer without your permission)

Interests and hobbies: . . . .   Positions held in any club or sport: . . . .

Declaration:

I do hereby declare that the information given on this application form is true and complete.

Signed: . . . .   Date: . . . .

This is an example of a Staff Application Form – type out your own on two A4 sheets, extending the boxes.

STAFF INTERVIEW QUESTIONNAIRE

The interviewer, not the applicant, should complete this form. Where there is an asterisk (*), please delete as necessary.

Applicant's Name: . . . .   Interview Date: . . . .

Application Form   *First, go through the form, requesting clarification of any point, then ask the following additional questions:*

1. When did you move to your present address? . . . .   2. Is the house: your own/rented privately/council/shared?*

3. Does your partner work?   Yes/No*   If Yes, what is their job? . . . .

4. *(If partner works and there are young children)* Who looks after your children during the day? . . . .

5. Are you in good health? Yes/No*   6. Do you smoke? Yes/No*   7. How many days were you off work this past year? . . . .

8. Who is your Next of Kin to contact in an emergency? *Name:* . . . .   *Relationship:* . . . .
   Address & Daytime Phone No.: . . . .

9. *(If applicant drives)* Do you own a car?   Yes/No*   10. Have you had any accidents or convictions? . . . .

11. Name, job title and address of two work references, plus bank. May we approach these for references?
    (1) . . . .
    (2) . . . .
    (3) . . . .

12. Are you prepared to work overtime/additional hours?   Yes/No*

Competence Tests *(Details of tests set and the results):* . . . .
. . . .
. . . .

Terms of Employment *(This forms the basis of information for the Job Offer letter)*

1. Job Title: . . . .   2. Job Start Date/Time: . . . .   3. Normal days/times for work: . . . .

4. Wage or Salary: £. . . . . per hr/day/week/month*   Paid by cash/cheque/direct credit*   5. Overtime/Bonuses? . . . .

6. Holiday entitlement: . . . .   7. Sick Pay discussed? Yes/No*   8. Pensions, if any, discussed? Yes/No*

9. Period of written notice req'd: . . . .   10. Disciplinary Rules discussed? Yes/No*   11. Grievance Procedure discussed? Yes/No

Interview Expenses

Amount Paid: £. . . . . . .   for: . . . .   Date Paid: . . . .

This is an example of an Interview Questionnaire. Photocopy it if you wish, using the reverse of the copy for additional notes

you would get some idea of how he or she operated under real conditions.

References Always check up on the references given. Often you get more information by phoning rather than writing to the referees. References from previous employers are very important as you want to know how the applicant performs at work. It is also relevant to know why they left their previous employers. Where an employee is likely to handle cash, a good idea is to ask for the applicant's bank as one reference (you will need to write to them as they are unlikely to answer a verbal request). Private character references from eg a vicar should be seen in the light that they have been selected by the applicant to reflect favourably.

Caution: When asked for a reference for a former employee, be very careful. If your reference is malevolent, this may give grounds for the employee to sue you and if it is inaccurate or untrue a subsequent employer may try to sue you. You have a duty of care to both parties.

Job Offer Letter Once you have found a suitable person and checked their references then you may wish to send them a letter offering them the job. It is a legal requirement to provide, in writing, the terms of employment for every employee, including part-timers, and this statement usually has to be provided soon after they join. Since the statement has to cover topics that should have been discussed at the interview the job offer letter and legally required statement might be combined – see the fictitious example on page 70. Please note that employment legislation has become very complex and you would be wise to get your solicitor to check your own Job Offer letter.

If the references have not yet been checked or the applicant has to have a medical examination, the letter could state *"this offer is conditional on satisfactory references (or medical report) being received"*. If you state the job offer is for a "trial" or "probationary" period then be sure to add that this can be terminated by statutory notice thus avoiding any possibility of a fixed term contract.

A suggestion is to attach a copy of the job offer letter with the added words: *"Signed as acceptance of the above offer and conditions"*. This makes it easier for candidates as all they have to do is read the job offer letter and if they agree, they can sign and return the copy, retaining the original.

It is good manners to write to all unsuccessful applicants but it is most unwise to explain why he or she has been rejected as that may give them cause to sue you on discriminatory grounds. So keep it polite but short.

EMPLOYMENT LEGISLATION

CAUTION **Please note this section is for general guidance only and should not be regarded as a complete or authoritative statement of the law.**

Payslip Each employee is entitled to be given a payslip with their wage packet or pay cheque. The payslip should itemise: gross pay, deductions (eg National Insurance, PAYE), variables (eg overtime, bonuses) and net pay. Where there are deductions, the amount, interval and purpose should be noted.

Unfair Dismissal Before dismissing anyone, do take professional advice. It is a tricky legal area. Grounds for dismissal include incompetence, misconduct or redundancy, but must be "fair and reasonable". An employee cannot normally claim unfair dismissal until he/she has worked for you for 2 years.

After 2 years, a dismissed employee is entitled, at their request, to receive a letter explaining why they are being dismissed and they are usually, though not always, entitled to a period of notice or payment-in-lieu (see **Giving Notice** on page 71).

Unless the employee is found guilty of gross misconduct such as stealing or assault, it would be good management practice to allow the employee adequate opportunity to change his or her ways – they should have had verbal then at least one, possibly two, written warnings, which should spell out: a) what they are doing wrong, b) what they must do to correct that and c) the consequences should they ignore the warnings. The second or "final written warning" as it is usually called should clearly state that no improvement or repetition will lead to dismissal. In addition you should have fully and fairly investigated the situation and allowed the employee to have his or her "say".

Where dismissal is in breach of contract, it is more likely to be a case of "wrongful dismissal".

Sex Discrimination Act and Equal Pay Act Remember that women have equal job opportunities to men and must be paid the same rate for the same job or for work of a broadly similar nature or equal value.

Health and Safety At Work This applies to employers, employees and the self-employed. If employing staff you should either give them each a

Worthless Products Ltd

Unit 3, Industrial Estate
Birmingham B1 1ZZ

Tel: 0121-123 456
Fax: 0121-123 789

Mrs C.A. Jones
Unlikely Avenue
Birmingham B1 1YY

26th September 1995

Dear Mrs Jones

Thanks for coming to the interview. We would like to offer you the position of Machine Operator, starting here at 0900hrs, Monday 16th October 1995.

Your duties will be the operation of the Widget Mk3 Machine and associated equipment and general assistance with the assembly of our products. You will be expected to undertake reasonable alternative duties at the request of management. You will be responsible to Mr Brown, the Production Manager. Your Main Terms and Conditions of Employment are as follows:

Pay: Your pay will be £.. per hour, paid weekly in arrears by cheque.

Overtime: The rate is .. once your normal daily hours have been worked.

Hours of Work: Normal hours of work are Monday to Friday, .. to ..hrs with one hour for lunch, which is usually .. to ..hrs.

Holidays: You will be entitled to .. weeks paid holiday/year plus public holidays.

Sickness: If you are sick you must notify the office within .. hours of your normal starting time. For illness lasting .. days or more, a Doctor's certificate is required. Statutory Sick Pay (SSP) will be paid from your .. day of sickness.

Pension: There is at present no company pension scheme. No contracting-out certificate under the Social Security Pensions Act is in force.

Discipline & Grievances: The disciplinary rules that apply to you can be found in the Company Handbook, a copy of which is enclosed. If you are dissatisfied with any disciplinary decision or wish to seek redress of any grievance relating to your job you should write to the Production Manager. Further steps following such an application are outlined in the Company Handbook.

Notice: You are required to give the company one week's written notice to terminate your employment. You are entitled to receive the following periods of notice: under 2 years service – 1 week; 2 or more years – an extra week for each complete year to a maximum of 12 weeks notice after 12 years service.

Please confirm by returning the copy letter with your acceptance and signature as soon as possible. If you have any queries please contact me. We look forward to you working here and hope you will find it rewarding.

Yours sincerely

J. Smith

John Smith
Admin. Manager

Manufacturers of Novelty Goods

Registered in England & Wales, Registration Number: 00000   Registered Office: Unit 3, Industrial Estate, Birmingham B1 1ZZ

This is a fictitious example illustrating how a business might send out a Job Offer letter. You should consider getting a solicitor to check your normal job offer letter.

copy of the leaflet "Health and Safety Law – What you should know", or display the poster. Every firm employing 5 or more people must, by law, write down its policy for their health and safety.

If you are a manufacturer you should contact the Health and Safety Executive at an early stage to establish what regulations are appropriate.

Statutory Sick Pay (SSP) There is a statutory requirement to pay a minimum level of sick pay for most employees who have been sick for 4 or more consecutive days. This is called Statutory Sick Pay. Full details are given in your PAYE "New Employers Starter Pack".

Maternity A woman employee has certain rights if she becomes pregnant. See the Department of Employment booklet PL 710 entitled "Employment rights for the expectant mother", and available from most Jobcentres.

Disability Discrimination Act This makes it unlawful to unjustifiably discriminate against a disabled person, but the Act only applies where there are 20 or more employees.

Confidentiality If your work involves trade secrets you may be able to get your employees to sign a non-disclosure agreement. This is best included as a clause in the terms of employment statement. Such a clause can prevent them from passing on information about your secret processes and the names of your customers. It can also prevent them competing directly against you but it cannot prevent them using their technical skill or trade knowledge to earn a living. This is a tricky area of law so requires expert professional advice.

Giving Notice After one month's continuous employment an employee is entitled to a minimum of 1 week's notice. From 2 years they are entitled to 1 week per complete year of service up to a maximum of 12 weeks notice for 12 years of service.

Guarantee Payments If you plan to temporarily lay-off staff due to a shortage of work, first read the Department of Employment's booklet PL 724 on "Guarantee Payments".

Redundancy This occurs when a firm wants to reduce its staff. The Department of Employment must be given at least 30 days notice if you plan to make more than 10 people redundant. Redundancy is only relevant if the employee concerned has been with you continuously for 2 years or more. Redundancy payments are calculated as so many weeks wage per year of employment depending on age and there is a maximum weekly pay value used in the calculation. The Department of Employment's booklet PL 808 gives more information.

Transfer of Undertakings If planning to buy or sell an existing business, note the Transfer of Undertakings (Protection of Employment) Regulations protects employee's jobs when a business is taken over.

GETTING HELP

For advice on most aspects of employment legislation, contact the nearest offices of ACAS (the Advisory, Conciliation and Arbitration Service). They have offices in Accrington, Birmingham, Bristol, Cardiff, Fleet, Glasgow, Leeds, Liverpool, London, Manchester, Newcastle and Nottingham.

FURTHER READING

ACAS publishes a useful handbook written for small firms, titled "**Employing People**". It costs £2 (plus £1 postage) and is available by post from ACAS Reader Ltd, tel: 01455 852225.

And available from most Jobcentres are free Employment Department booklets on a variety of specific employment legislation matters.

If you have a general question on tax, PAYE, National Insurance, SSP or Statutory Maternity Pay, phone the Employer's Helpline on: 0345 143 143.

A GENERAL COMMENT . . . .

Employing staff can present particular problems for a new small business. For instance, it can be difficult attracting high-calibre people to join a fledgling enterprise; unskilled or junior staff require a great deal of supervision and the paperwork related to employing staff is time-consuming. Finally, some proprietors have difficulty in accepting that their employees are likely to be less dedicated than themselves■

Doing Basic Officework

YOU may well loathe doing "paperwork" but it really is an essential part of every business venture, so here are some ideas on how to do it simply and effectively. There is also great satisfaction to be had from being organised and up-to-date with your paperwork.

OFFICE EQUIPMENT

You don't really need a new desk, executive high back chair or similar paraphernalia but what you may require is:

(1) a telephone; (2) a table used exclusively for your paperwork; (3) a comfortable chair to use at the table; (4) a filing cabinet (purchased second-hand if possible, and consider too if it should be fireproof); (5) a small electric typewriter or computer; (6) several clean cardboard boxes (approximately 12 by 9 inches) to temporarily file papers; (7) lots of blank A4 paper and other stationery items such as a stapler, paper clips, hole punch, ball pens etc and finally, (8) a cheap "IN" tray, "PENDING" tray and "OUT" tray for your table.

Always keep these costs down when starting a new business as they do not make profits!

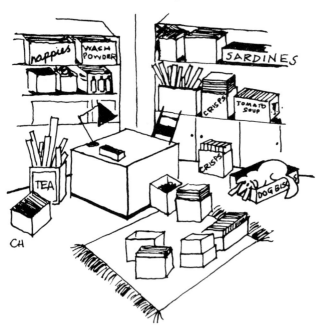

...... cardboard boxes to temporarily "file" papers.

Depending on the type of business you propose to start, you may need a photocopier. If so, consider purchasing a small one, rather than leasing, unless you are going to use it a great deal or need a more complex machine with reduction and collating facilities.

These days for many businesses it is almost essential to have a fax machine and increasingly the facility to send and receive e-mail too.

LETTERS

Handling incoming mail requires a certain amount of discipline. Whenever mail arrives always put it in the "IN" tray on your desk even before you open it, or place the mail in some other fixed location where it will not be mislaid. When you sit down to tackle the mail try to handle each letter or document once only ie do not open the envelope, scan the contents and put it aside to deal with later. Try to complete the task in one go.

If the content is an invoice, check it is correct, then put it on the Invoice Lever Arch File (this is explained in the chapter **Controlling The Finances**).

If the letter is a query of some sort that requires an answer, either: 1) phone (jotting down on the letter who you spoke to and what was said) or 2) write a note on the original letter, get a photocopy and post off the original letter with your note written on it or 3) type a letter in reply, keeping a copy. Use option 1) wherever possible for local addresses, option 2) for more distant addresses (comparing the cost of a telephone call to the cost of your time, a photocopy, envelope and stamp) and use option 3) where the matter is important and a proper written record is necessary.

Filing "Filing" is simply the grouping of similar letters and documents so you can find them easily at a later date. Grouping is normally done alphabetically A to Z in the same way as a Phone Book, so correspondence with a private customer, Mr Jim Scott, would be filed under "S" whereas correspondence with Mr John Smith, Administration Manager for Worthless Products Ltd would be filed under "W". Under "W" one would find any letters from Worthless Products Ltd and copies of letters from you to them. In addition to correspondence files you may have a few files for one-off or special subjects. For instance you may open a file, entitled "Raising Start-Up Finance" to enclose all correspondence, notes etc relating to that one topic.

TRING-A-LING ALARMS

Number 10
Sellers Lane
London EC1 1ZZ

Tel: 018-123 4567
Fax: 018-123 5678

Mr J. Smith, Manager
Worthless Products Ltd
Unit 3
Industrial Estate
Birmingham B1 1ZZ

6th June 1996

Dear Mr Smith

NEW RANGE OF SECURITY EQUIPMENT

This letter is to introduce our company which has been set up recently. We are offering businesses a comprehensive service of installing and maintaining security equipment.

The two partners behind Tring-A-Ling Alarms have between them over 20 years experience in the security field and have both worked for well-known companies in both technical and managerial capacities.

Tring-A-Ling Alarms can supply and fit locks, padlocks, window grilles and other physical security devices. We also install and maintain burglar alarms and closed-circuit television (CCTV). The latter can be of great use to management as it permits, for instance, observation of loading bay doors during the working day.

I would like the opportunity to meet you and to discuss your company's security equipment needs and I shall phone you in the near future to arrange an appointment.

Yours sincerely

A. Bell

A. Bell
Sales Manager

Experts In Security Systems
Partners: A. Bell, A. Clanger

This is a fictitious example illustrating how a company might send out a mailshot to get a sales appointment.

TRING-A-LING ALARMS

Number 10
Sellers Lane
London EC1 1ZZ

Tel: 018-123 4567
Fax: 018-123 5678

Mr J. Smith, Manager
Worthless Products Ltd
Unit 3
Industrial Estate
Birmingham B1 1ZZ

21st June 1996

Dear Mr Smith

WINDOW GRILLES – QUOTATION

Thank you for taking the time to meet me yesterday. I now have pleasure in providing you with a quote to supply and fit window security grilles for your factory.

Quantity: Four windows, all to the rear of the premises.

Specification: Mild steel expanded mesh as per sample left with you. Grilles to be attached to window surrounds by one-way security screws.

Price: £623.00 + VAT. This quotation is valid for 30 days.

Terms: Payment is due 30 days from date of invoice.

Guarantee: We guarantee our workmanship and materials for 12 months.

If you have any questions please do not hesitate to call me. I look forward to hearing from you in the near future.

Yours sincerely

A Bell

A. Bell
Sales Manager

Experts In Security Systems
Partners: A. Bell, A. Clanger

This is a fictitious example illustrating how a company might send out a quotation.

Doing Basic Officework

If you are unlikely to receive or generate much correspondence you could keep it all in a Lever Arch File (with stiff card A-Z separators) or an A-Z expanding pocket file. Otherwise you need to use conventional files.

Writing Business Letters

These should always be typed and you should keep a carbon copy (or photocopy) on file. A hand written letter looks totally unprofessional and would reflect badly on your business. If possible, letters should be written to a named person rather than a "Dear Sir" (which is less likely to get a response). Most letters consist of 4 parts:

1. Heading   This focuses the reader's mind. It should be in capitals and underlined.

2. Introduction   Normally one or two sentences describing the subject and referring, where applicable, to earlier correspondence or a meeting or phone call.

3. Main Body   This can be several sentences, several paragraphs (or in an extreme case, several pages!). It conveys the message of the letter. If it is a long letter or a quotation you can use sub-headings (or paragraph headings) as shown in the example opposite.

4. Actions   You have written the letter for a purpose. So in this final part of the letter there is a closing sentence or two stating what action(s) you want the reader to take and/or what action(s) you will be taking.

In a business letter one sometimes uses "we" unless you know the reader in which case it is more friendly to use "I". Finally, remember that if the letter is addressed as "Dear Sir" then it is signed "Yours faithfully" but if it is addressed as "Dear Mr Smith", it is signed "Yours sincerely". Refer to the two examples in this chapter which are first, from a new business trying to get work and second, a letter that is providing a quotation.

THE TELEPHONE

A great deal of business is done on the phone. Because phone bills can mount up alarmingly, try to make your calls, especially long distance calls, as short as possible (and ensure your staff do). If you are concerned about staff misuse of the phone, consider getting a small pay-phone. These can be rented or purchased and suit some types of small business, especially where customers can use it too (eg in a hairdressing salon, café or guest house).

Phone Techniques

Often the first contact a customer has with your business is the person who answers your phone. The customer's impression is therefore coloured by how they are treated on the phone and you may gain (or lose) a sale as a result. It is essential therefore to use a good phone technique . . .

1. Answering   When answering do not simply say "Hello" or give your phone number. Instead, try "Good morning, (then give your business name), can I help you?" or maybe "Hello, John Smith speaking . . .", or maybe give your business name first, followed by your own name. Whatever you decide to say, take time to say it clearly and do speak as if you mean it!

2. Recording Messages   Many problems occur when phone messages are not written down. Orders can get mislaid . . . complaints are not dealt with . . . new sales enquiries do not get followed up, etc. Pre-printed telephone message pads are available from stationers. Make certain each phone has a pad and pencil nearby and ensure the *name* and *number* of the caller is always recorded.

3. Calling   If phoning a business: (a) avoid calling between about 1200 and 1430 hours as whoever you want may be at lunch. Friday after 1530 hours can be equally difficult; (b) ask for someone by name or ask for a department. Most larger businesses have similar department names – Sales, Purchasing, Finance (also called Accounts), Production, Design, etc and (c) remember to say who you are and equally importantly remember to get the name and possibly the job title of the person you are talking to so you can make contact easily again by name. It is quite important to build up a good personal relationship with your business contacts. (Selling by telephone is mentioned more fully at the end of the next chapter).

Mobile Phones   No longer just a "yuppie" toy, these can be very useful if you are often away from your office and need to keep in touch or you are expecting calls from customers. Choose your service provider carefully as there are some unscrupulous operators around and keep calls short as it is an expensive form of communication.

Telephone Answering Machines If your office is left unattended for long periods and you are expecting calls, especially from potential customers, then a telephone answering machine would be a good investment■

Marketing and Sales

Y OU do not have a business unless you can make *sales* and the whole process of getting those sales involves proper *marketing*. Analysis of the market and assessing the competition are also parts of marketing and were covered in the chapter **Doing the Market Research**. Good marketing is vital to every business. When starting a new business the essential aspects are:

● Pricing your product or service.
● Advertising and promotion.
● Selling Techniques.

PRICING

Too few businesses do this properly! First, the meanings of two important terms ... "Fixed costs" (also called "overheads"). This refers to business expenditure which is basically constant, ie "fixed" irrespective of the level of trading. So for instance, rent, rates, most salaries, insurance etc are all fixed costs. Overheads must be kept to a minimum as they can soon overwhelm the profitability of a business.

Overheads ... can soon overwhelm the profitability of a business.

"Variable costs" – (also called "direct costs"). This refers to expenditure which varies directly in relation to the level of business, for instance, costs of raw materials or stock.

PRICING PRODUCTS

A straightforward way to price a product is as follows:

1. If you are a manufacturer   (This also applies to businesses such as catering where food products are made):

Selling price/unit =
(cost of raw material + direct labour + o/heads contribution) + mark-up + VAT

Cost of raw material: This should be relatively easy to calculate, but remember wastage. *Direct labour:* This is the realistic cost of employing staff to make the units, as shown in the following example. *Mark-up:* The mark-up (see also page 32) needs to be such that the manufactured items are sold at sufficient profit to cover the proprietors' or Directors' wages *plus* a small surplus (say 5-10%) to provide funds for future expansion, new product development or simply to save against any future contingencies.   *VAT:* This is only added if you are VAT-registered and the product itself is VAT rated. *Overhead contribution:* This considers the overheads of the business, which obviously have to be supported by the production. It assumes everything that is made is subsequently sold (an important point).

Overheads contribution = $\dfrac{\text{total overheads}}{\text{total production}}$

Example: Assume you are self-employed making either small craft products, electronic devices, garments or whatever. Assume also the raw materials cost £10/unit and each item takes 1 hour to make, so in a 40 hour week you could make 40 such items. Now in this equation what should you allow for your labour cost? One answer is to charge what you would have to pay an employee to do the job. Why? Because if your business expands and you take on someone, had you been basing your selling price on a low labour figure you would then either have to suddenly raise your prices or reduce your profits – both undesirable. Now, if an employee's wage is £200 per week, then allow about 33% more to work out the hourly rate – why? Because you have employers National Insurance contributions, plus paid holidays, plus sickness and higher overheads. So in this example the direct labour cost would be (£200 + 33%)/40 = £6.65/unit.

Next, assume total overheads (ie rent, rates, insurance, phone, heat, light) come to £8,000 and total annual production is 1,920 items (this assumes 48 weeks production, allowing you some holidays), then the overheads contribution/unit is £8,000/1920 = £4.17. Finally allow a mark-up of, say 10% (as you don't have any employees yet and the direct labour cost is in fact your "wage"), then the selling price is: (£10 + £6.65 + £4.17) + 10% = £22.90.

You might consider selling at £22.90 or a little more or less depending on the competition and the market.

In this example, the annual turnover (ie sales) = 1,920 x £22.90 = £43,968 which is below the current VAT threshold so the business would not need to be VAT registered and no VAT should be added to the cost.

KEY POINT Be cautious about pricing your product on the assumption that you will be operating at full production all the time for that is most unlikely.

2. If you are a wholesaler or retailer:

Selling price/unit = net cost price + mark-up + VAT (where applicable)

Example: If you buy an article for £4.65 net (ie without VAT added) and if the typical trade mark-up is 85% then the selling price = £4.65 + 85% + VAT which equals £10.11 (if the VAT rate is 17.5% and you are registered for VAT). There are four points to consider:

1. You may consider selling this article for £9.95 as that sounds more appealing to a customer.
2. Find out the typical trade mark-up percentages.
3. Keep your prices in line with your competitors.
4. Check the Cashflow Forecast reflects your mark-ups.

The effects of distribution on pricing How you distribute your product can make a great difference to your pricing, ie selling direct to a customer, using an agent on commission or distributing through a wholesaler or retailer can all make a difference. No way is best! Each is appropriate to a particular trade and you should know the mark-ups of the different distribution stages relevant to you so you can work out your "end-user" price to see if it is competitive. Some people when they start in business begrudge using wholesalers or retailers as they feel they will take too much profit. What they must realise is if they try to sell direct themselves it will take both time and promotion neither of which is cheap, and it might actually be better to sell indirectly through wholesalers or retailers who already have the outlets and the customers.

PRICING SERVICES

The pricing of services is normally based on hourly labour rates plus material costs. For consultancy or freelance work this is more usually called "fees plus expenses".

Calculating Hourly Labour Rates First of all find out typical "going rates" for what you are planning to do by asking people in the trade outside your area who are therefore not likely to be competitors. Next, if you plan to employ anyone, check that you can give them an adequate hourly wage out of that, making allowance for downtime and profit. Finally, insert that figure into your Cashflow Forecast by assuming you (and any employees) will be productive (ie doing work for which you can actually charge) for, say, 50% of the working week. The actual figure may be even lower and is unlikely to be much above 75%. By being productive for 50% means that in a typical 40 hour week you will only be charging for 20 hours but having to pay your staff for 40. The remaining 20 unproductive hours are absorbed in getting sales, doing paperwork, travelling, buying materials etc. If the Cashflow Forecast figure looks good and your labour rate is about that for the trade then that is a good start.

Materials These are usually charged "at cost" but if you charge your customer the same price that you paid, then you are ignoring the time you take to locate the materials, the cost of travel to collect them, the finance cost of materials held in stock, and so on. Some businesses define "at cost" as being the retail price whereas they purchase the goods at wholesale prices thereby giving themselves some margin.

Estimates and Quotations An "estimate" is the approximate price of something, but usually a buyer will ask for a "quotation" and in writing. A quotation is a fixed price and if agreed is binding on both parties. See the sample letter in the previous chapter. As all quotations involve a degree of guesswork, you should carefully record your actual expenditure on the contract (by simply noting each day what man-hours and materials were spent on the contract). In this way your guesses should get better with experience.

FURTHER READING The vital subject of Pricing is explored in greater depth in a companion book, "**The Greatest Sales & Marketing Book**" – see the end of this book for details.

Marketing and Sales

Advertising Method	Cost	Good Points	Bad Points
Direct mailshot letter	Low	Targeted audience. High response rate (2% to 5% or perhaps more).	Time consuming to carry out, as it takes time to locate or produce a good mailing list.
Small Poster	Low	Large readership. Long life.	Limited to where posters are allowed. Message must be short.
Letterbox leaflet	Low	Can be part-targeted. Low response rate (usually well under 1%).	Difficult to distribute effectively unless done by eg Post Office, which increases the cost.
Directories (eg Yellow Pages)	Low/Med	Advert life is 1yr. Allows comparison with competitors.	Can only make changes annually and ensure you use a relevant Directory.
Direct mailshot leaflet	Low/Med	Targeted audience. Response rate is highly variable.	Time consuming to carry out (but less time than personalised direct mailshot letter).
Advert in local newspaper	Med	Local audience. Can repeat often. Usually some supporting editorial is possible.	Readership much larger than your target. Advert has to compete for reader's attention. Today's news, tomorrow's fish & chip paper!
Advert in trade publication	Med/High	Targeted. Editorial may be possible. Long life. Often a Reader Enquiry Service.	If publication relevant, none, except price.
Advert on Local Radio	Med/High	Wide audience. Suits certain consumer and business markets.	Advert life very brief so needs repeating frequently.
Advert in national newspaper or magazine	High	National audience. Can repeat often. Colour usually available on some pages.	As per local paper and editorial mention less probable. Ensure likely sales will cover costs.
Advert in "glossy" magazine	High	Some targeting possible. Full colour available on most pages.	Need to book space months ahead. High cost of advert production.

ADVERTISING AND PROMOTION

You can have a desirable product or service to sell at an attractive price but if nobody knows about it your business will obviously fail! There are many ways of finding customers and even a small business should use a combination of these. Some ways are more costly than others while some are more effective. Cost and effect are not always clearly related! The different methods are basically:

1. Advertising.
2. Issuing Leaflets & Brochures.
3. Producing Press Releases.
4. Taking a Stand at an Exhibition.
5. Doing Special Promotions.

ADVERTISING

First we can consider advertising. There are many ways of advertising (see Box above). With all advertising one is trying to target the message at the person who actually buys. Before advertising in a newspaper, magazine or Directory check to see if similar firms are advertising, if not it may be the wrong medium for you.

People tend to suppose that because they had a large half-page advert in the local newspaper backed up with some editorial, now everyone knows about their business – WRONG! It is a sad reality but people forget adverts almost as soon as they have read them. This is *unless* they happen to have a need at the *precise* moment they see the advert, so you would probably have to advertise regularly, ie weekly (or monthly if it is a monthly publication), but you need not take large adverts, in fact a "little...often" is likely to give a better result than one or two big adverts.

Placing An Advert   For publications, phone the Advertising Department. Ask for their "advertising rates" which for the classified section will usually be quoted as cost/word or line and for display adverts are usually quoted as cost per single column centimetre (scc), which is a space one column wide and one centimetre deep. Display adverts are also quoted in terms of ⅛, ¼, ½ or full page. You should also ask by what date they need the advertisement. Ask them to send you a "rate card" which gives you all this information plus details of the circulation of the publication (ie how many people read it). If booking an advert, remember to send in a Press Release too (covered later in this chapter) as any editorial can be a great help.

Designing An Advert   Look at previous issues of the publication in which you plan to advertise and ask yourself — what catches the eye? It is very tempting to design an advert that seems to address itself to all readers — this is a "scattershot" approach and is rarely effective. Instead, address the advert to a specific section of the readership who will at least consider your product or service. Remember too the Trade Descriptions Act under which it is an offence to apply a false trade description to goods or services — in other words it must be honest and you must be able to prove any performance claims you make. Advertisments must never mislead.

If you are using a classified advert it needs a catchy heading. You can even take out two or more different adverts in the same issue — it is more effective than one long one. If you are placing a display advert remember a good photo or sketch is "worth a thousand words" so do use them. Remember too that as humans we respond most to photos showing people rather than inanimate objects.

Many new businesses give prominence in an advert to their company name but unless the name is very descriptive that is wasted for as a new business the name will have no impact, no meaning. However, if your company represents or sells a well-known brand name give that prominence (but do check first with the company concerned — they may even pay a portion of the advert). Another common error is to clutter the advert, yielding to the temptation to squeeze everything in. Remember the function of the advert is to arouse interest in specific readers and to encourage them to take the next step (eg visit you). This latter point can be emphasised in the advert by putting a closing date or using words demanding action. But avoid saying "Act now!" in an evening paper unless you plan to man your phones or whatever that evening! An effective style of display advert is the pseudo-editorial advert that looks and reads like a news item. Despite the words PAID ADVERTISEMENT at the top, if written skilfully, it can be very worthwhile.

Designing adverts demands time, skill and experience. It is all too easy to get it wrong and produce an advert that yields too few sales. The subject is covered in much greater depth in **"The (Greatest) Sales & Marketing Book"**.

KEY POINT   Slick advertising cannot sell a poor product or change the fate of a poor business.

LEAFLETS & BROCHURES

The purpose of a leaflet (pamphlet or brochure) is to convey a message in a lasting form. An advert in a newspaper or magazine will last only as long as the publication sits around (since most readers are too lazy to cut out an advert). Leaflets can also carry a much longer message than an advert. The design breaks down into several headings ...

Size   This is a function of the amount of information you need to convey, the intended method of distribution (eg envelope size) and the amount you can afford to spend. It is best kept to a standard size, typically A4 (210 x 297mm), A5 (half A4 in size) or ⅓A4. It can be flat or folded and can be printed on one side or both sides.

Colour   A full colour leaflet is expensive. It is only justified if the product or service you are offering is itself expensive or needs colour to fully show its features (eg a wallpaper leaflet would be worthless in black and white), or if it needs to be in colour to compete with a rival's full colour leaflet. Note that you only use "full colour" printing if you are incorporating colour photographs and the printing cost is related to the number of such photos. If full colour is not essential great effect can be achieved by using a 2 or even 3 or 4 colour print. Remember that each colour requires a separate printing operation and so increases the price. Be careful of printing black on a gaudy coloured paper as these are often used to advertise cheap products or services.

The headline promises a nice benefit and may therefore catch the attention of more prospective customers than a specific heading eg "Garden Furniture".

Photos and illustrations are more convincing than words. Ensure scenes are lively and include people.

An introductory comment is required which clearly explains what is on offer.

The main part elaborates on the offer. Remember to add prices and give enough product information to arouse interest.

A call for action by an incentive is always useful.

If space permits you might advertise more of your range but never jeopardise the main offer by over-crowding.

Your business name would not normally be given emphasis unless it is particularly descriptive as to what you do.

Make the most of Summer with your Family and Friends

(space for colour photo, which extends under the heading above to create a large splash of colour. In this example the photo might show the furniture outside in the sun with a few happy people around and the heading above could be printed over the sky).

Garden Furniture — Huge Stock!

We can now offer a complete choice of attractive, comfortable and yet affordable garden furniture in pine, aluminium or plastic. Elegantly designed and carefully made to be enjoyed and admired. Chairs from £19.95, tables from £49.95.

Special Offer: 20% discount if you bring this leaflet and buy at least one table and 4 chairs before 31st May 1996.

We also stock a full range of pots, potting mixes, tools, seed, hoses, fertilisers, gravel, seedling trays, sprays, plants, greenhouses........

John Smith Garden Centre
Rose Street, Anytown
Tel: 017-234 5678

For the Greenest of Gardens

(Fictitious Example)

This leaflet would probably require printing in colour to maximise its impact.

A little white space helps avoid the cramped, crowded look.

If your leaflet has a lot of text, it is important to arrange it in well spaced blocks so that it is easy to read. Prospective customers will not stop to read text which needs deciphering.

A map may be important when you are not located in a town centre site or are hard to find.

If you have a business slogan or motto you could add it.

Material   One can print on thin paper or thicker card with either matt, semi-matt or gloss finish. The thicker the paper the more expensive it is but it does have a better feel.

Information   A leaflet should read like a letter:

1. Heading. To focus the reader's mind. This is in large type and can either be descriptive, eg GARDEN FURNITURE or questioning, eg NEED SMART NEW GARDEN FURNITURE? or assertive, eg GARDEN FURNITURE NOW IN STOCK or indicating a benefit, eg MAKE THE MOST OF SUMMER WITH YOUR FAMILY AND FRIENDS.

2. Introduction. Normally a short paragraph explaining the heading.

3. Main Body. This could be several paragraphs or even several pages but do remember your reader may be a busy person so keep it as short as possible and try to make it interesting.

4. Call For Action. You are producing the leaflet because you want it to trigger some reaction. The end of the leaflet should therefore urge the reader to do something, such as contact you – by phone or letter, so your address and phone number should be given clearly. As we are all lazy and hate writing letters a simple reply coupon is useful.

Design   For any leaflet to achieve maximum effect the design must be good and it is suggested that professional help be sought when drafting it.

Folder   This is a specialised style of "leaflet", suitable where you are dealing with a small customer base, say under 100 or so, and the product or service you are supplying is complex or changing. The idea is to print a smart folder of lightweight card, usually A4 in size. Into this folder you can slip photocopied sheets of information, possibly an introductory letter and, where applicable, photographs. The folder gives impact to your presentation while maintaining maximum flexibility, by allowing you to add to or change the information sheets within it.

Distributing Leaflets This is very dependent upon your product or service and who are your likely customers. Here are some alternative ways of distributing leaflets:

a) Post through letter boxes (business addresses or homes).

b) Use the Post Office to deliver (they currently charge £40 per thousand 20g leaflets, with a minimum charge of £100).

c) Insert as loose in newspaper or magazine (they charge for this). Particularly popular with trade publications.

d) If your target market is local consumers, your local newsagent may, for a small charge, include them with the paper round.

e) Hand out in the street or at special events that attract your type of customer (but check if you need permission).

PRODUCING PRESS RELEASES

See the example over the page. It can be very worthwhile sending a Press Release to all relevant publications whenever you have something that is newsworthy. Include clear black and white photographs (they prefer 5x7 inch or 6x8 inch photographs) if possible featuring people because the human element is important to the media. If sending a photo remember to type a clear description of what the photo shows (especially the names of people) and stick the description to the back of the photo.

In Press Releases do *not* use superlatives or make suspect claims (eg "...the world's cheapest..."). Also, as shown in the example, quotes from relevant people are appreciated. Journalists prefer warning of events but if you do not want premature publicity you can use an embargo note on the top of the Press Release – this is a polite request to the publication not to print anything on the subject until the date shown on the embargo.

A good piece of editorial is worth a dozen adverts but do remember that: a) the publication may or may not use your news item, b) they may choose to use it days/weeks later, and you have no control over that, and c) they will write the article in their own words and with their own bias which may not be to your liking!

Trade publications are more likely to use your editorial than the consumer press but here are a number of hints to increase the chances of your Press Release being used: (a) Try to tie-in your news with some bigger event or story that the publication is already running; (b) Keep the Press Release short (under a page) and written to catch the eye and hold the reader's interest; (c) Put the most important aspect in the first paragraph (as any editing is usually done from the bottom up); (d) If available, a good photograph often helps and (e) Follow up the Press Release by phoning the appropriate Editorial department – not always a popular strategy but it can work.

SIMPLY PERFECT

12 Regent Crescent
Greenock
PA1 1ZZ

Tel: Greenock (01475) 242

PRESS RELEASE

NOT FOR PUBLICATION
OR BROADCAST BEFORE
2ND MAY 1996

LAUNCH OF NEW FASHION VENTURE IN GREENOCK

At a short ceremony in Greenock today, Petunia Smart, the well-known actress, opened the new fashion boutique called SIMPLY PERFECT.

The shop, located at 12 Regent Crescent in Greenock, will stock ladies outerwear for the mature successful woman. The range will include chic dresses, attractive skirts with many co-ordinating blouses, dashing coats, head-turning hats and an extravaganza of accessories.

Joan Smith, 42, the proprietor of the new shop and a former teacher, said "At present many ladies cannot find smart outfits locally, I hope this new shop will meet their needs". Joan has visited the fashion houses in London, Paris and Milan to select her stock.

TV Personality, Miss Smart, who lives in the town said "I always need to dress well for my television appearances and I will certainly be making use of SIMPLY PERFECT. I spotted some nice Italian blouses with floral prints".

The Director of the local Enterprise Agency, Mr Helpful, said "We are delighted to have been able to assist Joan Smith with this venture. We helped her prepare her Business Plan and provided other advice. This is the 250th new business start-up that we have helped this year".

To introduce the stock to local clientele, there will be a fashion show at the Golfing Hotel on the 20th May. Free tickets are available from the shop.

PHOTOGRAPH attached

FOR MORE INFORMATION:

Contact: Joan Smith
Tel: Greenock (01475) 242

Proprietor: Joan Smith

Shop Hours: Mon-Sat 9.30am - 5.30pm

This is a fictitious example of a Press Release, typed on the shop's normal letterhead.

EXHIBITIONS & OTHER PROMOTIONS

Exhibitions.. Participating in Exhibitions, Consumer Shows and Trade Shows has become of increasing importance. For non-retail businesses they provide regional, national or even international exposure. However, many new exhibitors are disappointed with the results of their initial showings. This is mainly due to inexperience and unrealistically high expectations. (It might also be, one should add, that their product or service is not viable.)

Exhibiting requires a great deal of preparation, an adequate budget and hard work before, during and afterwards to make the most of it. The decision to participate should not be made on the spur of the moment.

Essential preparation includes: a) visiting a number of similar exhibitions and talking to the organisers; b) deciding which show(s) to exhibit at; c) designing stands; d) organising leaflets and exhibits; e) deciding on any supporting publicity to encourage people to visit you; f) working out manning rosters and booking accommodation; g) reading the fine print of the exhibition rules and h) training staff how to sell effectively from the Stand.

Seminars/Talks/Demonstrations These can be very useful if you get the *right* audience. It can be used for many different businesses including both manufacturing and service industries. You need to think carefully who your likely buyers might be then invite them to an occasion where you can have their attention and give them your sales "pitch".

If you are selling to trade buyers then you may be able to tag on to some other event (eg a trade association or Chamber of Commerce meeting). If not, to get the buyers to come you need to make the occasion sound interesting and appealing − perhaps lunch or drinks at a nice hotel may encourage them to come.

If you are going to this effort to set up such an important occasion you should ensure that your presentation is good, ie a good speaker, good visual aids (maybe a video or slides), samples on display and leaflets for people to take away. If possible try to have a full rehearsal beforehand.

Monitoring Your Advertising & Promotion Whatever method of advertising or promotion you use, as it is costing you time and money you should monitor the results. For leaflets or newspaper adverts one can say something like "Bring this leaflet (or advert) to get 10% off" or with leaflets an idea is to make a secret mark on several of the leaflets distributed with a note on the leaflet that whoever brings in a leaflet so marked will get a (desirable) gift.

Where the buyer has to write, as in mail order, an old trick is to use a fictional department in the address so you know that replies addressed to "Dept M" were in response to a certain advert. If you are actually meeting customers (eg in a retail situation), ask politely how they heard about you.

With all monitoring write down and analyse the results. Here is a fictitious example for a shop:

68 customers were asked how they knew about the new shop of whom 12 people (18%) saw an advert in the local newspaper, 15 people (22%) heard about the shop by word-of-mouth, 26 people (38%) were just passing the door and came in and 15 (22%) were already repeat customers.

SELLING TECHNIQUES

There is a saying that customers "buy benefits, not goods or services". What that means is best illustrated by an example. A soccer fan may buy a video recorder because he wants the benefit of being able to replay his favourite matches. If there was some other way he could do that he might not be buying a video recorder. In other words it is not really the video recorder he needs and is buying, but the benefit it gives him. It is worth bearing the concept in mind when you are trying to sell something.

This section covers successful selling techniques which, if applied, will help you overcome any fears you might have and will assist you achieving that essential ingredient of all businesses − more sales!

Remember too (and remind staff) that it is your customers who provide your income and your staff's wages − so make customers feel important − they are!

1. FACE-TO-FACE SELLING (NON-RETAIL)

This could be "cold calling", ie you do not have an appointment or it could be a pre-arranged meeting. In any event, before you set out: (a) dress smartly; (b) gather adequate sales material and know it thoroughly; (c) have price lists to hand and (d) leave on time so as not to be late.

Sales material is a key element of face-to-face selling. It consists of samples, brochures, your business cards, order forms and possibly a calculator if you need to come up with estimates or quotations on the spot. If you do not have a

Marketing and Sales

good brochure and it is not possible to carry samples due to their size, an effective substitute is a photo album with clear pockets into which you slip a piece of blank paper onto which are fixed photos with a typed description. The photo album can also contain newspaper cuttings, letters of commendation (testimonials), certificates of technical competence and so on. Of course you need not show every page to every customer.

Handling The Meeting Here are some tips for the actual sales meeting:

* There is no need to be nervous as people enjoy chatting and you have an excellent product (or service) to sell.

* Don't run up stairs or along corridors as it will make you out of breath.

* Don't have a drink beforehand to steady your nerves as the smell can be noticed and gives a poor impression.

* On meeting the "prospect" give a firm handshake and hand over your business card if you've not met before.

* In a business context, if you are not sure of the "prospect's" name or job, ask for his or her business card.

* Listen to find out the customer's *needs*. If you can match those needs, explain how your product or service can achieve that.

* If the customer raises objections, this is healthy and the objections should be listened to carefully. It may help you to jot down what is said so you can overcome objections one at a time without missing any.

* Close the sale, get the buyer to sign a copy of the order form and leave them a duplicate copy of the order which should include the agreed price and timescales.

Note: The Consumer Protection (Cancellation of Contracts Concluded away from Business Premises) Regulations 1987 provide for a 7-day cooling off period in which agreements covered by these Regulations can be cancelled by the consumer. Get a leaflet from your Trading Standards Officer.

Techniques For Closing The Sale You must learn to be able to sense when a customer is ready to buy — he or she may start to ask detailed questions or talk about methods of payment. Then you can attempt to close the sale by, for instance:

1. Take out your order book (very visibly) and ask something like "so, how many **** do you want in your first order?" or "on what date would you like your first order delivered?" (and then discuss quantities).

2. Another technique is to bypass the yes/no decision completely by discussing details of the order, getting the customer involved and then take out your order book.

If the customer says he needs to "sleep on the matter" before he decides, then leave something like your personal catalogue (marked ONLY COPY) or samples which you arrange to collect the next day (or the day after, ie don't let it cool too far!). This tactic allows you to see the customer face-to-face again which gives you a second opportunity to close the sale and it is much more difficult for the customer to turn you down in person, than over a phone.

If the customer is unsure because he needs a boss's or colleague's opinion, ask for that colleague/boss to join your discussions or arrange to come back and see them all (ie try not to let them decide in your absence!).

If the customer says he needs to sleep on the matter ... leave your samples ...?

2. FACE-TO-FACE SELLING (RETAIL)

Small retail outlets fall into two categories — "convenience shops" (such as a newsagent, corner shop or chemist) and "specialist shops" (such as a boutique, gift shop or TV and electrical shop). In a convenience shop the customer tends to make most of his or her purchasing decision *before* they enter and in a specialist shop the customer tends to make his or her decision *after* they enter. That is a crude simplification but it emphasises the differences in selling. In the former case there is little "selling" as one is primarily responding to the customer's requests, though selling can still play a part by encouraging the customer to buy additional (often complementary) purchases.

Let us concentrate though on the specialist shops where selling plays a greater role. Here are some suggestions:

1. Always acknowledge the presence of a customer very soon after they enter the shop, by a nod, smile and possibly a "Hello" or "Good Morning" even if you are already dealing with another customer. This makes them feel more at home on unfamiliar territory (especially if they have not visited the shop before) and it also tends to "hold" them until you are free to help them. It is a simple strategy and yet ignored by many shops.

2. Let the customer browse for a few moments and then approach them. Do not say "Can I help you?" as you will get the universal reply "No, I'm just looking!" which stops your sales pitch dead in its tracks. Instead, try using a question more related to the situation. For instance, if a lady is looking at blouses, you might ask "Is the blouse to match a particular skirt?...what colour?...day wear or evening wear?...". In a gift shop, you might ask "Is it something for yourself or a birthday present?...". The point of these questions is they tend to open up a dialogue which has several advantages: a) it stops the customer rushing around the shop and disappearing out the door, b) it allows you to find out what the customer *needs*, c) it allows you to offer your goods to match those needs and d) the customer will think you are being helpful. On the other hand, being too pushy can of course lose sales.

3. The show window is a crucial factor in selling from a specialist shop. The window is the magnet that draws people in (very often on an impulse) so it should be bright (actually lit up with lots of lights), attractive and articles on display should be clearly priced. The window should be changed weekly or fortnightly and it should have a theme such as a subject or a common colour. For ideas, look at the windows of the big department stores (who all have full-time professional window dressers) and take notes to use for your own shop.

4. Sales material you should have includes showcards and posters or stickers which are produced by the suppliers of the stock you are carrying. They may also provide leaflets.

5. Layout. The shop layout is important to assist your selling and should be discussed with shopfitters who know about retailing your type of goods. In particular, thought should be given to point-of-sale displays as these can contribute significantly to your turnover.

3. TELEPHONE SELLING

The telephone is a most useful tool to back up your sales drive, however to use it effectively requires skill and practice. There are courses available for tele-sales techniques which could be worth attending. The main advantages of selling by phone are: a) you can contact a large number of people in a relatively short time and b) you can often get through to the decision maker. Its main disadvantages are: a) you cannot show your product or other sales material to the customer and b) you cannot see their facial reactions.

As with any sales work, preparation is essential, so you must know who you are calling and what you are trying to achieve with the call. The phone conversation should be handled in very much the same way as any sales meeting so in your opening statement you would identify yourself and your company. You should also state clearly what is the purpose of your call. This opening statement should be rehearsed but not recited parrot-fashion. So should your fact-finding questions and sales message. Several other hints are as follows:

1. Try to keep a smile on your face.
2. Keep your product/sales information in front of you.
3. Remember the customer will be thinking "What's in this for me?"
4. Understanding the customer's business is half the battle.
5. Close the sale, or where appropriate, arrange an appointment to see the customer.
6. Since there is nothing in writing, always summarise what has been agreed and later confirm in writing if necessary.
7. Bear rebuffs bravely — don't get rude or angry.
8. Pause then put the phone down after the other person.
9. Keep a record of all your calls■

Exporting

WHY export? Businesses start to export for different reasons, but the main one is usually the desire to make the most of a good product or service that is applicable to a wider market than just the UK. Another good reason to try exporting is to ultimately have your eggs in more than one basket. But exporting is not usually a solution for a business that is having difficulty selling its products in the UK.

Some companies actively pursue an export policy and produce a Business Plan with that venture in mind, while other companies slip into exporting because they have been approached by an overseas buyer and this slowly leads to other export sales.

Government, naturally enough, tries to encourage exports, but the proprietor of a small business cannot afford to be dazzled by the sales pitch. Also, though there is much promotion of the European Single Market, there are of course many important markets outwith Europe, notably North America. As a small business it may be wise to focus initially on one small export area rather than trying to take on the whole world!

Who Should Think of Exporting?

First of all, a small company should probably not consider exporting unless either the company is well established in its home market making it financially strong enough to set out on this new adventure or one of the proprietors has been in this field before and "knows the ropes". This therefore does not exclude new or recently started businesses.

Exporting can be exciting, though the initial glamour of jetting around the world and staying in hotels etc can wear thin. It certainly can provide enormous opportunities even for the smallest of businesses − provided they have the right things to sell.

Exporting, however, is not something to simply dabble in!

GETTING INTO EXPORT

Market Research As with any new business venture, the first thing to do is to find out more about the market, ie to do some market research. There are people who can help (speak to your Enterprise Agency or business development unit), but one good and quick way is to visit an appropriate trade show in the country concerned. Speak to people in the trade over there and get copies of relevant foreign trade publications (from which you can have selected articles translated later).

It may be that your product will require modifying to suit specific overseas markets. Find out too if you will require an import licence for the country concerned, if there are any import duties and if you require an export licence from the UK (such licences are needed only for a limited range of items).

Distribution Assuming your market research results are encouraging, for

---

Some Advantages of Exporting

Market Size Obviously one of the biggest advantages is the potential market is larger than simply this country.

Market Match The product or service you are selling might suit certain overseas markets better than the UK.

Eggs in several baskets Selling in markets beyond the UK provides a possible "hedge" against a downturn in this economy.

Currency Advantage Although outwith your control, a change in currency exchange rates can give you a definite selling advantage if Sterling is weak against your customer's currency.

Some Disadvantages of Exporting

High Costs It's very expensive travelling abroad to get orders. Expensive in management time too. It's also expensive shipping goods and paying Agent's fees which raises your prices and may make them uncompetitive.

Market Mismatch Culture, customs and language can all be different to what you are used to − sometimes quite alien. This has the practical problem that a successful product or service in the UK might be of little use or interest to people abroad.

Regulations Obviously you need to know what local regulations apply. There may also be import restrictions or onerous duties.

Shipping Procedures There is a lot to learn!

Currency Disadvantage It was mentioned above that a fluctuation in exchange rates can be beneficial, equally it might not be!

Unpaid Debts A potential problem facing businesses which export is collecting debts. This can be a very serious problem.

manufacturers you need to consider the options to market your product:

1. Agent. An agent will visit potential customers, take orders (usually on a 10% commission) and then you ship the goods direct to the customer and invoice these customers direct. Finding a good, reliable agent and controlling customer debt are the main problems.

2. Distributor. A distributor not only goes out taking orders but also stocks your goods. You then only have to ship goods to (and invoice) the distributor. As with agents, they should not only sell your goods but also provide important feedback from customers.

One way to find an agent or distributor is by recommendation through your trade association. Alternatively the Department of Trade and Industry operate the "Export Representative Service" which for a fee will provide a list of possible representatives.

3. Sell Direct. This can be done by taking a Stand at a Trade Show abroad or by visiting selected customers. Just as with the first option above, you would have to ship and invoice each customer individually. Follow up sales might be difficult or just too expensive for you to undertake, unless you have potentially big customers who will order in sufficient quantity to make a trip worthwhile.

4. Collaborative Projects. A completely different approach is some form of collaboration with an overseas company. This might take the form of you providing certain facilities or contacts for them in exchange for them providing the same for you.

5. Manufacture Under Licence. In this case an overseas manufacturer agrees

Here's the supply boat .... I wonder what today's exchange rate is for coconuts?

to make and sell your product locally. You could supply parts to them or even the whole product in kit form. Alternatively you may just get paid a royalty. This is complex legally and needs good advice. It is essential to fully check-out the other party's track record, financial status and integrity.

Services: The above options are mainly for manufacturers. For a service business, the options depend very much on the type of business concerned.

Trade Shows Even the smallest business can consider participating in international Trade Shows. First it is useful to go as a visitor to assess the Show and the competition. For selected overseas Trade Shows there may be some grant assistance available from the DTI for new exporters.

There are, of course, international Trade Shows held in the UK which

attract foreign buyers and a business can make a tentative move into exporting by exhibiting at one of these.

If looking for an agent or distributor abroad, you might display a small sign "Agent Wanted" in your Stand.

If you plan to make your contacts through an annual overseas Trade Show, a good rule-of-thumb is the first year you will not make enough sales to cover your costs, the second year you may, with luck, break even and in the third year you may achieve profit.

Pricing A major problem with exports is the extra costs that inevitably make your products more expensive abroad than they would be if selling at home. Even if you are selling on an "ex-factory" or "fob" basis, the end price of the goods will still be higher.

These additional costs include freight charges (and the often onerous handling and shipping agent fees); shipping insurance (always more expensive than when simply moving the goods within the UK); export credit insurance; import duties where applicable; and bank charges. There might also be an overseas agent's commission to add.

Hence a product which retails in the UK for £10 (with a 100% mark-up for the retailer) might be the equivalent of £12, £15 or more, on the shelves in another country. This can obviously diminish the appeal of your product unless the foreign economy can withstand the higher price or if the currency conversion is in your favour.

How To Send Goods For most products there are probably three options. The first option (if the goods are lightweight) is by post. This can be by air (which is relatively expensive but quick) or surface (which is cheaper but takes

Exporting

many weeks to most places). One big advantage is that you have no handling agent's fees, so for small orders this can be quite useful.

However, most exporters will have to consider using the two other options — air freight or sea freight. A good Shipping Agent is essential to handle the often complicated documentation and to advise on the best route and carrier — the most direct way is not always the best. If you are quoted a shipping cost in terms of £/kg (quite often its $/kg), then remember to ask about the handling charges which can add quite a lot to the overall bill.

ARRANGING PAYMENT

It is one thing to succeed in getting an export order, it is quite another matter to actually get paid for it! Certain countries seem to be notorious non-payers while others have the reputation of being excellent payers. Expert advice is required and this is available from the DTI's Export Credits Guarantee Department, 2 Exchange Tower, Harbour Exchange Sq., London E14 9GS, tel: 0171-512 7000.

Whereas with a UK customer you might insist on payment by proforma (ie they pay before you send the goods)

the normal method for an unknown export customer is to use either a Letter of Credit or other documentary collection, which are handled through your bank and are relatively safe.

If you plan to offer credit, do remember to take up references just as you do with any UK customer.

Note that a bank will charge not only to arrange the transfer of cash (by eg Letter of Credit) but will also charge to convert a foreign currency payment into Sterling. To avoid the latter you could ask your customer if they can pay by "Sterling cheque drawn on a UK bank" — and if they are unable to do this then ask your bank what their conversion charges are likely to be.

AND FINALLY

If you are seriously considering exporting, as a first step you should speak to your local Business Link, Business Shop, or other local business development unit.

Note: If you are VAT registered and you want to trade with other EC states, you will soon discover that there is additional VAT accounting to be done and more returns to be completed■

KEEPING GOING!

Chapters

BUSINESS is all about money, and the proper management of that money is paramount to the success of any business. This chapter covers the operation of a business bank account, keeping records, how to keep a simple set of accounts and how to do Cashflow Management (as based on the Cashflow Forecast you did for your Business Plan).

I said PROPHETS Isaiah, not PROFITS !

Business . . . is all about money

BUSINESS BANK ACCOUNT

The first principle to grasp is that it is vital to separate "business" money from "personal" money. It is rather like when a friend asks you to buy something for them and gives you a £5 note. You put this money in a separate pocket and after buying the item you return the change to that pocket keeping it apart from your own money – it is a simple discipline that prevents any embarrassing confusion. In a business context this separation is achieved by opening a business bank account and keeping any loose cash from the business in its own container which can be either a cash till or tin box clearly marked "Business".

Opening An Account   You will need to make an appointment to see your Bank Manager to discuss opening the business account. The manager will want to know about the intended business, so you should be prepared – take along a copy of the Business Plan you have already completed.

In addition to wanting to know all about your proposed venture, the manager will usually ask some of the following questions:

Account Title   This is the name which is normally printed on your cheques. If it is a limited company, then it is normally the company title in full. For a sole trader or partnership it can be the personal name(s) with, it is suggested, the words BUSINESS A/C added, eg JOHN SMITH BUSINESS A/C. When a business name is to be used you could just have the trading name, eg TRING-A-LING ALARMS but it may be better to have the proprietor's name(s) added like this: A. BELL & A. CLANGER T/A TRING-A-LING ALARMS ("T/A" just means "Trading As").

Signatures   The bank will also ask who can be an authorised signatory to the bank account. If it is a partnership or there are two directors (in the case of a limited company) then the bank will want to know if one signature or two will be necessary on cheques and other authorisations. In this case it may be wiser to require two signatures for each cheque or the bank could be instructed not to pass any cheque over some specified amount, unless there are two signatures.

Statements   The bank will wish to know how often you want to receive a bank statement (monthly is the most usual and is recommended). They will also need to know to which address the statement should be sent.

Bank Finance   The manager will want to know if you will be looking to the bank for finance. If this is the case then you should leave a copy of your Business Plan at the bank several days before your appointment to give the manager time to read it.

Opening Deposit   Finally, to get the new account open, the bank will normally request a deposit of money from your personal funds.

Writing Cheques   Cheques are often written out very carelessly with the high risk of either the cheque being tampered with or the bank innocently debiting a wrong amount.

It is wise to "cross" your cheques with two bold diagonal lines and the words *A/c Payee Only* (your cheques may already be pre-printed as such).

Also if you have to give someone a blank cheque then write clearly somewhere on the cheque *Amount not to exceed £25* (or whatever value is relevant).

It is vital to keep track of the value of the cheques you have written. If your cheque book has stubs, one good tip is to write on the next unused cheque stub the total amount left in the account after writing each cheque. This means you are always aware of how much is left and you are never in danger of overdrawing the account – but watch out for direct debits and credits which will affect the balance.

One last point on the subject of cheque writing and it may seem like

Controlling the Finances

stating the obvious, but it is absolutely crazy to write a cheque when there are no funds in the bank account (it is also an offence!). The repercussions of this folly can be horrific – the bank will "bounce" the cheque and your lines of credit will dry up as suppliers become nervous. Worse still, your bank will think that you are unable to control your finances and they may withdraw any overdraft facility you might have – with potentially terminal results for your business.

Handling Money   Many new businesses that handle actual cash create difficulties for themselves when cash received from customers is used partly for business purposes and partly for purely personal items, with no proper records being kept.

A good habit is to pay all the money you receive (ie cash and cheques) into your business bank account. When you want to "pay" yourself you write a cheque to yourself, and if you need to buy something for the business you would normally pay by cheque. But if you are only buying something costing say, less than £10, then you have two options:

1. Petty Cash   Writing cheques for small amounts is not only a time consuming exercise but potentially expensive in bank charges. If you think you may need to buy a total of £50 of small purchases, then you could cash a cheque for £50. Put the money into your "petty cash box", buy the items you need, get receipts for everything and keep a note in the appropriate columns of your Accounts Book.

2. No Petty Cash   Alternatively, as illustrated below, use your own money for the various purchases, keeping the receipts. Then at the end of every week or month you total up the receipts and write yourself one cheque, made out to "Cash", to reimburse your private pocket for the purchases.

Unless your business involves a great deal of buying small items, the second method is preferable as it involves less paperwork and effort.

Bank Statements   Each month the bank should send you a statement. Statements should be filed neatly together and kept in a safe place as your accountant will want to see them when doing your annual Tax Return.

The statements should always be checked: a) to ensure the correct amounts have been credited and debited; b) to verify what bank charges and other D/Ds (Direct Debits) have been deducted and c) to see that any direct credits have indeed been paid into your account.

The Direct Debits and any Direct Credits should be written up without delay in the Accounts Book and the running total on your cheque book stub should be updated too.

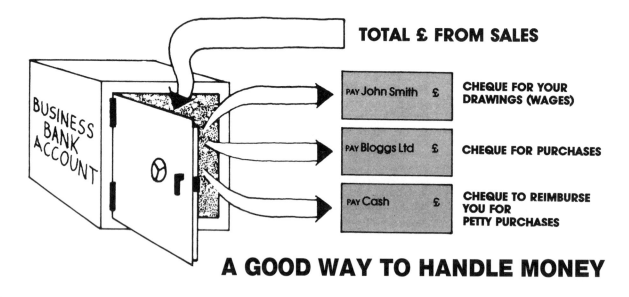

TOTAL £ FROM SALES

PAY John Smith £ — **CHEQUE FOR YOUR DRAWINGS (WAGES)**

PAY Bloggs Ltd £ — **CHEQUE FOR PURCHASES**

PAY Cash £ — **CHEQUE TO REIMBURSE YOU FOR PETTY PURCHASES**

A GOOD WAY TO HANDLE MONEY

KEEPING RECORDS

Keeping Receipts (Invoices) You need to keep the receipts for *everything* you buy in connection with your business. Despite using the word "receipt", an "invoice" is usually acceptable and more common when payment is made by cheque. Here for simplicity we shall just use the word "invoice" to mean both.

Invoices should be filed in some manner. One suggestion is to keep the invoices paid by Petty Cash in an envelope (one for each month) and to use a 2-hole lever arch file for the invoices paid by cheque, as shown right. Cheque invoices should be filed in *cheque number* sequence. Write the cheque number boldly on an outside corner of the invoice so that it can be cross-referred to easily.

You can use a card divider in the lever arch file to separate *paid* from *unpaid* invoices. File unpaid invoices on one side of the card, and when you pay them, move them to the other side of the card. This should prevent you from forgetting to pay any bills.

Rather than simply using an envelope for your Petty Cash invoices you could use another 2-hole lever arch file, but in this case the invoices would be filed in *date order* and simply numbered in sequence starting from 001.

The purpose of keeping receipts (ie invoices) is so that you have proof of purchase and can justify those expenses to the taxman. Note that a proper invoice should give the supplier's name and address, date, amount and a proper description of the goods or service supplied. It should also have an identifying number. Other than for small amounts, it should also give the purchaser's business name.

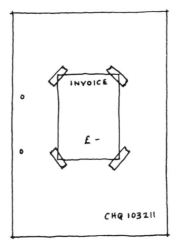

A receipt (invoice) which is too small to fit the Lever Arch file can be mounted first on a piece of blank A4 paper.

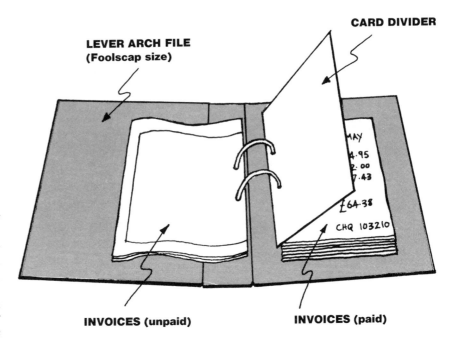

LEVER ARCH FILE (Foolscap size)

CARD DIVIDER

INVOICES (unpaid)

INVOICES (paid)

Controlling the Finances

If VAT-registered, invoices must show additional information – please refer to page 106 in the next chapter.

KEY POINT Keep receipts for everything, even before you start trading.

If you begin to buy a lot of goods or services on credit then you may find it difficult to keep track. A solution is to start a book called a "Purchase Ledger", an example of which is shown opposite. You could either buy a lined hardcover book and draw your own columns or you could buy loose-leaf pre-printed ledger pages, but in either event only record what you have to.

Keeping A Record Of Sales In every business you should have a record of your sales as proof for the tax or VAT inspector, and for your own information. In a shop, this record could be the cash till roll, while in other businesses it could be a duplicate copy of all the invoices you issue. These invoices could be produced on your computer or you could type them on a letterhead or you might hand write them using a duplicate invoice book (available from any stationers).

If you are offering credit, ie not being paid immediately, you should have a record of who owes you, how much, and how long the bill has been unpaid. This record is called a "Sales Ledger" and one suggested layout is shown opposite. As with the Purchase Ledger it could simply be a hardcover book with your own columns drawn on it.

Additional Records You must also retain your business bank statements, pay-in books, cheque book stubs, orders and delivery notes, relevant business correspondence, import and export documents, copies of any credit/debit notes and a list of goods taken from the business for personal use or supplied to someone else in exchange for goods or services. In addition, if you transfer any money between your business and personal bank or building society accounts, then you must also retain those statements. You must also record all purchases or sales of assets used in your business. Ask your accountant in advance what records he or she will want to see at the end of your tax year. (Note: If you employ staff, you will need to keep records relating to PAYE).

KEEPING SIMPLE ACCOUNTS

You may be hoping your accountant will "do the books" for you. This is not ideal for two reasons. First, and most importantly, knowing your exact financial situation is essential to managing your business and if you or one of your staff keeps the books then you ought to know what is happening. Second, using an accountant to do your book-keeping will be expensive.

When you *should* use an accountant is: a) for advice before and in the early stages of setting up the business, b) to

---

USEFUL GLOSSARY

Credit Note Can look like an invoice (and hence confusing) but is in fact an I.O.U.. Issued if, for example, a customer returns faulty goods.

Delivery Note A contents slip included with goods that are delivered or collected (usually on credit).

Input Tax (If you are VAT-registered). This is the VAT you pay on your business purchases and expenses, and which you can normally reclaim.

Invoice The bill you get when you buy something, or the bill you issue to your customers. Called a "tax invoice" if it involves VAT.

Output Tax (If you are VAT-registered). This is the VAT you charge your customers when you make "taxable supplies".

Receipt A slip confirming payment. Not often issued these days if payment is made by cheque, but useful when payment is by cash.

Remittance Advice A slip (often sent with a Statement to a customer) which the customer then returns with their cheque.

Statement A summary of invoices issued and payments received. Normally issued monthly to a customer who is buying on credit.

Taxable Supplies (If you are VAT-registered). Are those business transactions that are liable to VAT. Those not liable are called "Exempt Supplies".

Tax Period (If you are VAT-registered). The period covered by a VAT Return, usually 3 months.

Tax Point (If you are VAT-registered). This is the "time of supply" and is usually when the goods were supplied or a service is completed.

VAT Fraction (If you are VAT-registered). If a total includes VAT, then multiplying the total by the VAT fraction will give the amount of VAT.

PURCHASE & SALES LEDGERS

Notes:

1. Use one page per supplier/customer.
2. File suppliers pages together — these form the PURCHASE LEDGER.
3. File customers pages together — these form the SALES LEDGER.
4. A ledger is like a bank account statement, so in a Purchase Ledger when you buy £75 of goods this is shown in the "Credit" column and when you pay your suppliers the payment is shown in the "Debit" column.
5. In contrast, with a Sales Ledger, when you sell £50 of goods this is shown in the "Debit" column and when it is paid for by the customer their payment is shown in the "Credit" column.
6. (*) In the column below marked "Ordered By" you could use a single letter to indicate how the order was placed, eg T — placed by telephone, L — placed by letter and V — a verbal instruction.

PURCHASE LEDGER

Suppliers Name: .... Your Account No: ....

Address: .... Credit Limit: £ ....

Tel. No: .... Any Special Factors: ....

Contact: Mr/Mrs/Miss .... Job Title: ....

Date	Your Order No.	Ordered By (*)	Description	Goods Received	Invoice Received	Debit	Credit	Balance	Notes

SALES LEDGER

Customers Name: .... Account No: ....

Address: .... Credit Limit: £ ....

Tel. No: .... Any Special Factors: ....

Contact: Mr/Mrs/Miss .... Job Title: ....

Date	Customer Order No.	Ordered By (*)	Description	Goods Sent	Invoice Sent	Debit	Credit	Balance	Notes

Controlling the Finances

help create your book-keeping system, c) for taxation advice once the business is started, d) to do your annual accounts and Tax Return and e) if necessary, to help you raise money for expansion.

BOOK-KEEPING SYSTEMS

Keep It Simple! There are many different ways of keeping accounts and any way is acceptable provided you, your accountant, the tax man and (if registered for VAT) the VAT man, can understand it! It is essential that you yourself understand the system as some small businesses have failed partly because their book-keeping system was so complex that the proprietor could not understand it.

Single Book or Multi-Ledger? When you start in business you will probably only need to keep a single Accounts Book, but as your business grows you may need to consider moving to more complex (and expensive) systems. Usually the move to a multi-ledger system occurs not because your turnover has reached any particular level but because you need more "control" of purchases and sales made on credit, which in practice usually means the control of slow-paying customers.

Not surprisingly, operating a multi-ledger system takes much more time and effort as it involves double-entry book-keeping, and its users usually ultimately consider computerising their accounts.

Multi-ledger accounts systems are outwith the scope of this book as they are usually of less relevance to a new-start small business.

Single Accounts Book Systems

Every business needs an Accounts Book to record the funds received and payments being made. It is sometimes

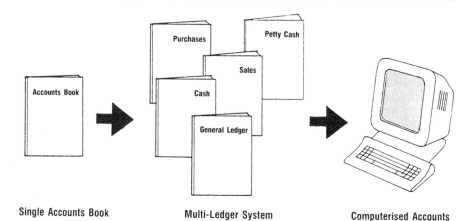

FROM A SIMPLE ONE-BOOK "SYSTEM" TO MORE COMPLEX SYSTEMS AS A BUSINESS GROWS

referred to as a Cash Book and it should relate to the bank statements, sales receipts and purchase invoices.

There are a number of single Accounts Books designed for the smaller business. The books fall into two categories: (i) those which are pre-printed so the user only has to fill in the figures where directed (like the example opposite) or (ii) "blank" accounts books which are merely ruled with lines and columns but have no headings or instructions and therefore require some knowledge of book-keeping.

ACCOUNTS BOOKS

First we look at some pre-printed Accounts Books on the market:

1. The Best Small Business Accounts Books (Price about £8.95 and available from main branches of W.H. Smith or Ryman's or mail-order direct from Hingston Publishing. See the end of this book for ordering details).

These two Accounts Books are from the publishers of "The Greatest Little Business Book". They are intended to be the simplest and easiest to follow

on the market and have been designed specifically for non-VAT registered small businesses (see page 98 for a VAT version).

Different types of business need different designs of accounts books and hence there are two in this series.

They have colour coded covers – the YELLOW BOOK is for a *cash business with daily sales* and is ideal for small shops, many self-employed, driving instructors, market traders etc. A page from the YELLOW BOOK is shown opposite (reduced in size) and there is one such page for each week of the year.

The BLUE BOOK is for a *credit business where sales are mainly invoiced*. It is ideal for small manufacturers, consultants, freelancers, agents, tradesmen, importers, builders etc. Pages from the BLUE BOOK are shown on pages 100-102 (reduced in size). There are four pages to each month.

Other businesses such as guest houses, office service businesses, craft-workers, caterers, vehicle repairers etc. can choose whichever book best suits their style of operation.

The Best Small Business Accounts Books

These books are for non-VAT registered businesses. One book is for a *cash* business and its cover is colour-coded YELLOW. The other book is for a *credit* business and its cover is colour-coded BLUE.

The illustration (right) is a fictitious example given in the YELLOW BOOK. As you can see, all weekly transactions are recorded on one page.

Normally A4 (210 x 297mm) in size the page has been reduced to fit here.

Week 1 commencing 6th May

MONEY RECORD

	£	p
Money in hand at start of week	178	23

DAILY TAKINGS

	£	p
Monday	63	12
Tuesday	39	73
Wednesday	127	32
Thursday	98	40
Friday	122	43
Saturday	163	82
Sunday		
Total Takings	614	82

OTHER MONEY, LOANS etc

	£	p
Cash from Bank	50	00
From Private a/c	1000	00
Total	1050	00

WEEK'S MONEY BALANCE

	£	p
Money at start of week plus Daily Takings plus Other Money, Loans etc	1843	05
Less Total Bankings	1571	71
Less Cash Payments	161	02
Leaves: Balance	110	32
Money in hand at end of week	110	22
Discrepancy ±	–	10p

BANK RECORD

	£	p
Bank Balance at start of week	841	27

DAILY BANKINGS

	£	p
Monday	158	23
Tuesday		
Wednesday	80	65
Thursday		
Friday	1332	83
Saturday		
Sunday		
Total Bankings	1571	71

BANK DIRECT DEBITS etc

	£	p
Cashed Cheques	50	00
Charges/Interest	34	75
HP/Lease/Loan		
Total	84	75

WEEK'S BANK BALANCE

	£	p
Bank Balance at start of week plus Daily Bankings less Bank Direct Debits plus Bank Credits	2328	23
Less Chq Payments	1920	21
Leaves: Balance	408	02

BANK STATEMENT CHECK

	£	p
Balance (from above)	408	02
Not yet on Statement: Add total cheques	1509	00
Less total bankings	1332	83
Leaves:	584	19

PAYMENTS RECORD

	PAID BY CASH			PAID BY CHEQUE		
	Ref	£	p	Ref	£	p
Stock/Raw Materials						
A. Jones	133	22	20			
A. Supply Co				072	87	23
I.M. Quick	134	12	32			
Brown & Son				073	107	24
J. Smith Ltd				076	156	90
Stock/Raw Materials Sub-Total		34	52		351	37
Advertising/Promotion						
Business Insurances						
Cleaning						
Drawings/Salaries/NI/Pension						
Self	140	80	00			
Electric/Gas/Heat Elec				074	23	79
Fees (eg Accountant, Lawyer)						
Motor – Fuel				079	9	00
– Repairs/Service						
– Tax/Insurance						
Postage/Parcels	136	1	12			
Rates						
Rent						
Repairs/Maintenance						
Staff Wages						
B. Good				075	22	60
A. Helper	139	40	00			
Staff PAYE/NI						
Stationery/Printing	137	3	50			
Sundries 135 56p 138 £1.32		1	88			
Telephone/Fax						
Travelling						
Other Expenses						
Refund Customer (by post)				077	13	45
CAPITAL EXPENDITURE						
Van (2nd hand)				078	1500	00
Total Cash & Cheque Payments		161	02		1920	21

© 1991 P. Hingston

Controlling the Finances

In both the YELLOW and BLUE BOOK there are full instructions and worked examples. A special feature is their "self-balancing" columns. These make it much easier to calculate the money and bank balances.

At the end of each book are simple summary sheets to complete at the end of the tax year. An accountant would need these in order to complete the Tax Return. The *Best Small Business Accounts Books* are suitable for Sole Traders, Partnerships or Limited Companies.

For PC Computer Users:
The Best Small Business Accounts Software *(Available only by mail-order – see page 119).* This software mimics the Accounts Books, so for the YELLOW BOOK a file represents a week and the screen shows a similar layout to that in the book. Similarly with the BLUE BOOK's monthly pages. The programs are basic so they are easy to understand and you could be up and running in about an hour or so – no heavy manuals to wade through, no long learning curve. This simple software runs on most PCs (not Apple Macs) from a 286 upwards.

2. The Best VAT Business Accounts Book *(Price about £9.95 + VAT, available from main branches of W.H. Smith or Ryman's or mail-order direct from Hingston Publishing. See page 119).*
To complement the *Best Small Business Accounts Books*, there is a self-contained VAT version of the BLUE BOOK. With a similar format but with additional columns for VAT and a new section to list VAT Inputs and Outputs. The VAT Account has been specially designed to make the completion of VAT Returns much easier.

3. The Simplex D *(Available from most stationers, price about £9.95).* This book is primarily for small non-VAT registered businesses which have transactions, ie purchases or sales, almost daily. The book provides one page per week

and contains instructions and example specimen pages. There are also end-of-year summary sheets at the rear.

If using a *Simplex D* and you need to register for VAT then you can use their special *Simplex VAT Record Book* in conjunction with the *Simplex D*.

4. Collins Complete Traders Account Book *(Available from most stationers, price about £17).* This is designed for VAT-registered shops. It contains instructions and example specimen pages. The book also has sections to permit you to calculate and record your VAT. Collins also produce the similar *Self-employed Account Book* for businesses not concerned with cash retailing.

5. The Twinlock Complete Accounts Book *(Available from most stationers, price about £16).* This is an accounts book suitable for many VAT-registered businesses. It is a loose-leaf binder style of book which has the advantage that you can add sheets. It has instructions and worked examples.

Blank Heading, Ruled Accounts Books
Pre-printed accounts books as mentioned so far can be used by virtually anyone without book-keeping experience (with a little coaching from their accountant or business counsellor). In contrast, the blank heading, ruled type of accounts book requires someone with suitable book-keeping knowledge to set up and may be more difficult for the novice to comprehend. However, once mastered, they are more flexible.

Available from most stationers are the **Cathedral, Guildhall** and **Cambridge Analysis** books, priced from about £10 to nearly £20 (depending on size).

These books are suitable for both VAT and non-VAT registered businesses and come in different sizes (A4, A3.5 and A3), in different thicknesses (ie with more

pages) and most importantly, with differing numbers of columns. Choose a book with enough columns to suit your business – your accountant can advise you.

AT YEAR END
At the "year end" there are important, but relatively simple, additional tasks to carry out. *Note:* The "year end" refers to the end of your financial (tax) year, rather than the calendar year.

For instance, if you hold any stock, raw material or part-completed work, you need to do a stock-take on the last day of your financial year. A "stock-take" involves counting all the different items you have and valuing them (normally at cost price). Another task is to list all your business creditors (ie people you owe money to) and debtors (ie people who owe you money) as of that date.

Some of the better pre-printed accounts books have suitable pages and instructions to help you with these end of year tasks.

COMMON BOOK-KEEPING PROBLEMS
Typical problems you might encounter when doing your book-keeping, include:

(1) If you are a sole trader or partner and use your private car or home telephone partly for business use, then you could pay these bills by business cheque, keeping a record of the business usage and at the end of your tax year you should be able to claim that proportion of the expenses; (2) If you pay for any business items using your personal credit card, when the card statement arrives, simply pay for the business items using a business cheque; (3) If you are unsure if an invoice is regarded as a "business" expense, either ask your accountant or note it on the appropriate page of your accounts book; (4) If you trade as a sole-trader or partnership and want to transfer some surplus cash into a deposit account, then enter it in the accounts book under

Controlling the Finances

"Drawings" (even if you plan to take the money back into the business later); (5) If you are using one of the blank heading, ruled accounts books, you may wonder what column headings to use. This question is best answered by your accountant.

Two other points: If a figure in your accounts is negative (eg a bank balance in overdraft) this is normally shown by brackets, eg (£100) means -£100. Second, if you are *not* VAT-registered, then throughout the accounts book you should record the full invoice value, inclusive of any VAT charged.

And Finally . . . .
Do try very hard to keep your book-keeping up-to-date. Don't give up!

CASHFLOW MANAGEMENT

The Objective One of the most common reasons a small business gets itself into financial trouble is due to "cashflow problems". This usually occurs when goods (or services) are bought on credit and later when the bills come in there is no money (or overdraft facility) to meet those bills. Cashflow problems may result from the business being under-capitalised, having low sales figures or suffering from bad payers. Even a profitable business can still have cashflow problems if its customers are slow in paying or it is expanding faster than its available capital allows.

In every business, cash comes in . . . . . but so do the bills and it can soon become difficult to control. This is where Cashflow Management is useful as it helps you to forecast your future cash requirements and any problems can be spotted early and something done about it.

Cashflow Management is in fact a very simple technique and once mastered you will really wonder how anyone can run a business without it.

How Does It Work? You will have prepared a Cashflow Forecast for your business before you start (or you ought to have!). Have a look at the Cashflow Forecast prepared for the fictitious shop "Simply Perfect" on page 44.

If this was your business, then at the end of the first month shown on the cashflow (May in this example) you would add up the actual amounts under the different headings in your Accounts Book (which should match the headings being used in your cashflow) and insert those into the cashflow. See right.

Very quickly you can spot that the May sales were much lower than forecast (£605 actual instead of £1000 forecast). So you would revise downwards your June forecast to perhaps £1000. The net effect is that the likely overdraft by the end of June is going to reach £2,483 unless urgent action is taken – and action is necessary since the overdraft limit is only £2,000.

If this was your own shop, the action you would have to take might include cutting back on stock purchases and talking to the bank about temporarily increasing your overdraft limit. But the key question is why are the sales lower than anticipated and what can be done about that?

Returning to the cashflow, each month you would update it as follows: first, insert the actual figures for the month just passed, then look at the months ahead and update your earlier forecast. Now check your bottom line does not either go into the red or exceed your overdraft limit. Using any spreadsheet program on a computer makes this work considerably easier.

Finally, never confuse cash *inflow* with *profitability*. Money sitting in your shop's cash till or your bank account may be needed to cover bills. And remember that the bottom line of a Cashflow Forecast represents neither a "profit" nor a "loss" ∎

Cashflow for fictitious shop "Simply Perfect"

	CASH IN	MAY	JUN
1	Sales (inc VAT)	605	1000
2	Bank or other Loans		2000
3	Owner's Capital	6500	
4	Other Money In		
5	TOTAL	7105	3000
	CASH OUT (inc VAT)		
6	Stock/Raw Materials	5122	3000
7	Advertising & Promotion	187	
8	Bank Charges/Interest		
9	Business Insurance	350	
10	Drawings/Salaries/NI		300
11	Electric/Gas/Heat		75
12	Fees (eg Accountant, Lawyer)	300	
13	HP/Lease/Loan Payments		80
14	Motor – Fuel		
15	– Other Expenses		
16	Postage/Carriage		
17	Rent & Rates	1000	250
18	Repairs & Maintenance		50
19	Staff Wages		
20	Staff PAYE/NI		
21	Stationery/Printing	31	
22	Sundries	96	50
23	Telephone/Fax	248	50
24	Travelling		
25	VAT		
26	Other Expenses		
27	CAPITAL EXPENDITURE	1263	136
28	TOTAL	8597	3991
29	Net Cashflow	(1492)	(991)
30	Opening Balance	0	(1492)
31	CLOSING BALANCE	(1492)	(2483)

© 1991 P. Hingston

99

The Best Small Business Accounts Books

These are accounts books for non-VAT registered businesses. One book is for a *cash* business and its cover is colour-coded YELLOW. The other book is for a *credit* business and its cover is colour-coded BLUE.

The illustration (right) is a fictitious example given in the BLUE BOOK. Each month has 4 pages and these are shown (in reduced size) on this and the following two pages.

The BLUE BOOK is now available in a VAT VERSION (not shown here). The layout of the BLUE VAT BOOK is the same as the non-VAT version except there are additional columns for VAT, an extra 32 page VAT section and help to complete your VAT Returns.

Normally A4 (210 x 297mm) in size the page has been reduced to fit here.

Month 1
month & year ...... **March 1996**

© 1991 P. Hingston

SALES RECORD

Date of Invoice	Date Paid	Customer	Invoice Number	Invoice Total £	p
4		John Smith Ltd	026	82	75
5	4/5	B.I.G. Buyers & Co	027	962	43
8		Brown & Son	028	165	00
12		A. Supply Co	029	96	37
16	3/5	ABC Co	030	15	25
17		D. Jones	031	85	50
19		B.I.G. Buyers & Co	032	650	00
23		Brown & Son — CREDIT NOTE	033	(15	00)
23		D. Jones	034	23	15
~~26~~		~~A. Supply Co~~	~~035~~	~~90~~	~~00~~
26		A. Supply Co	036	95	00
31		ABC Co	037	160	26
31		John Smith Ltd	038	104	84
		Total		2425	55

SALES RECORD (continued)

Date of Invoice	Date Paid	Customer	Invoice Number	Invoice Total £	p

BANK RECORD

Bank Balance at start of Month				£	p
				1505	64

BANKINGS			Non-Sales		Sales	
Date	Details	Ref	£	p	£	p
4	Sales	136			220	48
8	From Building Soc'y a/c	137	1000	00		
11	Sales	138			382	50
19	Sales	139			955	25
26	Sales	140			986	60
31	Sales (Brown & Son) Invs 028/033				150	00
	Direct Credits **ABC Co** Inv 015				126	50
Totals			1000	00	2821	33
Total Bankings (ie Total Non-Sales + Sales Bankings)					3821	33

BANK DIRECT DEBITS etc					
Date	Details		Ref	£	p
26	Bank Charges/Interest	*Quarterly Charge*		65	00
1	HP/Lease/Loan repayments	*Car loan*		145	00
Total				210	00

MONTH'S BANK BALANCE & STATEMENT CHECK			
Balance at start of Month + Total Bankings − Direct Debits		5116	97
Less Total Cheque Payments (total from overpage)		4491	52
Leaves: Balance at end of Month		625	45
BANK STATEMENT CHECK	Add total cheques not yet on Statement	400	00
	Less total bankings not yet on Statement	1136	60
	Leaves: Balance as per Statement	(111	15)

PETTY CASH

© 1991 P. Hingston

Money in Petty Cash at start of Month			£	p
			37	34

MONEY INTRODUCED DURING MONTH					
Date	Source of Money		Ref	£	p
4	From Bank account	Chq	359	50	00
19	From Bank account	Chq	368	50	00
Total				100	00

PAYMENTS BY PETTY CASH		£	p
Stock/Raw Materials			
Advertising/Promotion			
Cleaning			
Drawings/Salaries			
Electric/Gas/Heat			
Motor − Fuel	£18 £15 £9 £12	54	00
− Other Expenses	*Repair*	29	99
Postage/Parcels	98p £5 £6.50	12	48
Rent/Rates			
Repairs/Maintenance			
Staff Wages			
	A. Helper	20	00
Stationery/Printing		6	75
Sundries			56
Telephone/Fax			
Travelling			
Any Other Expenses	*Trade magazine*	2	00
Total Payments by Petty Cash		125	78

MONTH'S PETTY CASH BALANCE		£	p
Petty Cash at start of Month + Money Introduced		137	34
Less Total Payments by Petty Cash		125	78
Less any surplus Cash paid into Bank			
Leaves: Money in Petty Cash at end of Month		11	56

Only a few entries are shown here to illustrate how these pages might be completed.

Please Turn Over ▷

Month 1 ... March ... PAYMENTS BY CHEQUE (Note: There are overflow pages after Month 12)   © 1991 P. Hingston

Date	Cheque Paid To	Chq No	TOTAL		Stock/ Raw Material		Advertising/ Promotion		Drawings/Sal/ NI/Pension		Electric/ Gas/Heat		All Motor Expenses		Postage/ Parcels			Rent/ Rates		Staff Wages & PAYE/NI		Stationery/ Printing		Sundries	
3	Auto Repair Co	357	70	05									70	05											
4	Self	358	100	00					100	00															
4	To Petty Cash	359	50	00																					
5	Paper Supplies Co	360	17	50																				17	50
8	ABC Co	361	128	26																		128	26		
9	The Phone Co	362	189	87																					
10	A. Landlord	363	500	00														500	00						
12	Petrol Station	364	139	99									139	99											
12	Parcel Services	365	158	27											158	27									
15	A. Brown	366	562	58			562	58																	
16	Computer Supplies Co	367	2125	00																					
19	To Petty Cash	368	50	00																					
25	Self	369	400	00					400	00															
Total Cheque Payments for Month			4491	52			562	58	500	00			210	04	158	27			500	00			128	26	17	50

THIS chapter is to help you to cope with Income Tax (including PAYE), National Insurance contributions, Corporation Tax and VAT.

Note that these are not the only taxes that might confront you – for instance there is Capital Gains Tax and Business Rates which could apply. See the handy **Tax Data Page** at the end of this book and get professional advice from a qualified accountant.

CAUTION Please note this chapter is for general guidance only and should not be regarded as a complete or authoritative statement on taxation. For more information, please consult an accountant, the Inland Revenue, Contributions Agency or HM Customs & Excise.

WHO PAYS WHICH TAXES?

Depending upon the legal form of a business and whether or not there are employees, dictates which taxes are relevant and how these taxes are collected. So who pays what?

Sole Trader or Partnership (with no employees) In this case Income Tax is based on the business profits as declared in the annual Self Assessment Tax Return, and the Income Tax is paid in instalments (currently in January and July each year).

In the case of new partnerships, the profits of the business are divided equally between the partners unless the Partnership Agreement says something to the contrary. Each partner is liable only for the tax due on his or her share of the partnership's profits.

In addition to Income Tax, a sole trader or partner is liable to pay Class 2 National Insurance contributions (which are a fixed weekly amount) and Class 4 contributions (which are profit related and calculated as a percentage of the profits in your Tax Return). Class 4 contributions are collected the same time as Income Tax. The Class 2 contributions are best paid by direct debit through your bank.

Sole Trader or Partnership (with employees) In addition to the above, if you have any employee who earns more than a certain amount then you must deduct National Insurance (and pay an Employers contribution). If they earn more than a certain (higher) amount then PAYE (Pay-As-You-Earn) also has to be operated so that Income Tax can be deducted from their wages. The operation of PAYE is illustrated on pages 108 and 109.

Limited Company If you are a salaried Director you will almost always have to operate the PAYE system for yourself as well as any full-time staff you employ. Normally you need to pay Income Tax and National Insurance contributions monthly. Note there are special rules for calculating Director's National Insurance contributions, in particular, Directors have an annual earnings period – refer to the manual CA44(NI35) which should be included with your "New Employers Starter Pack".

In addition to these taxes a limited company is also liable to Corporation Tax which is a tax on profits, paid usually 9 months after the accounting period.

Cars and Fuel As an employer, if you provide a car or fuel for a Director or higher-paid employee's private use, you may be liable to pay Class 1A National Insurance contributions.

THE DIFFERENT BUSINESS TAXES

We now consider each of the main taxes in turn . . . .

INCOME TAX
(For Sole Traders or Partnerships)
Consider this example: assume your total annual sales (ie "turnover") is £50,000 but you had to spend £40,000 on stock, staff wages, rent/rates and other overheads, then you would have made a profit of £10,000. That would be declared in your Tax Return and the £10,000 is then regarded as the equivalent of a wage of £10,000. You are still entitled to your normal "personal allowances" and what is left is taxed at the prevailing rate of Income Tax.

If it's any help your horoscope says "It's time to run wild and free and be at peace with the world ..."!

Coping with Taxation

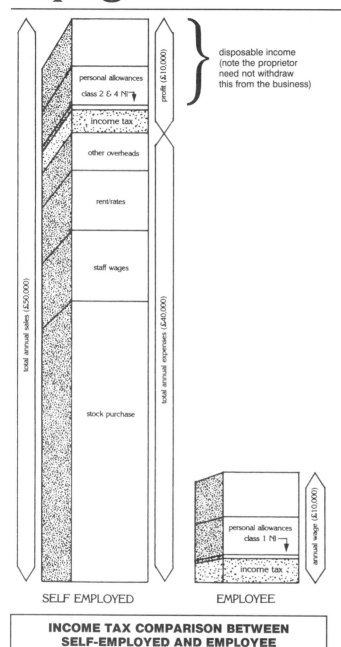

personal allowances

class 2 & 4 NI

income tax

other overheads

rent/rates

staff wages

stock purchase

total annual sales (£50,000)

profit (£10,000)

disposable income
(note the proprietor
need not withdraw
this from the business)

total annual expenses (£40,000)

SELF EMPLOYED

personal allowances

class 1 NI

income tax

annual wage (£10,000)

EMPLOYEE

**INCOME TAX COMPARISON BETWEEN
SELF-EMPLOYED AND EMPLOYEE**

Note that it makes no difference how much money you actually draw from the business – £25 per week or £250 per week, as your liability to Income Tax is solely dependent upon the *profitability* of your business!

The example we have discussed is shown graphically on the left.

Allowances In the above example we deducted £40,000 in costs from the £50,000 annual sales figure to arrive at the profit figure of £10,000 on which income tax is due. But what types of expenditure and "overheads" can you deduct? For income tax purposes an important distinction is made between "revenue expenditure" and "capital expenditure". Broadly speaking, "revenue expenditure" covers consumables and wages which would all normally be allowable deductions. This includes purchasing of stock or raw materials, staff wages, business rent and rates, phone bills, electricity and heating charges, advertising, stationery, insurance, professional fees, the replacement of worn-out tools by similar tools, necessary repairs and maintenance, interest on business loans and most vehicle expenses.

"Capital expenditure" covers once-off purchases of tangible assets such as business premises (including alterations), equipment, tools and vehicles. These are *not* automatically allowable – only certain categories are allowable, which are given a general writing-down capital allowance, which is currently 25%.

Only revenue expenditure which is *wholly and exclusively* for your business can be deducted from your annual sales figure when calculating your taxable profits. Items that are *not* allowable for income tax purposes include: your own drawings (ie your "wages"), household food or other domestic expenditure, Income Tax, business entertainment etc.

Use of domestic phone or vehicle There are frequently situations with small businesses where expenditure is partly for business and partly for domestic purposes. Examples include the use of a car, the use of a telephone at your home and heat and lighting used in an "office" in your home. In the case of a car (or van) you could keep a vehicle log book in which you record every business trip (ie Date, Destination, Mileage and Purpose of Journey). In the case of a telephone you could also keep a simplified log of all business calls you make to back-up an itemised phone bill (if available). In this way you will have the necessary proof to claim the correct proportion of the charges against tax. But before you start to log anything, do speak to your accountant as you may be giving yourself an unnecessary burden.

Construction Industry 714 Tax Certificate   If you plan to work self-employed as a sub-contractor in the construction industry you may need to apply for this certificate. Without such a certificate the main contractor has to deduct tax at the basic rate from all payments and this may make obtaining sub-contract work difficult. Contact your local Inland Revenue office for more details.

Coping With Income Tax   Provided you keep accounts, as suggested in the chapter **Controlling the Finances**, and you use an accountant to advise you, then you should be able to cope. The Inland Revenue's pamphlet IR28 is very readable and provides good advice for sole traders and partnerships. Remember to keep money aside to pay your tax! If your turnover is low, the Inland Revenue will accept simplified "three line accounts" (see the **Tax Data Page** at the end of this book).

NATIONAL INSURANCE
(For Sole Traders or Partnerships)
Even if you are already in employment and paying Class 1 National Insurance contributions, if you start a small business you may still need to pay a Class 2 contribution as well. However, if your self-employed earnings are less than what is called the "Small Earnings Exception", no Class 2 stamp need be paid. Refer to the **Tax Data Page** at the end of this book and if you are in this category, then contact your nearest Social Security office for more information.

Class 2 National Insurance contributions are paid separately to Class 1 so even if you employ someone, you will still have to pay your own Class 2 contributions separately (employees pay Class 1 contributions – see **PAYE** below). Visit your nearest Social Security office and ask for the appropriate leaflets for a self-employed person. You can elect to pay your Class 2 contributions monthly by direct debit from your bank account.

The Class 4 contribution which is based on the profitability of your business is generally assessed and collected by the Inland Revenue at the same time as your Income Tax. The Class 4 contribution is calculated as a percentage of the profits exceeding a certain figure but there is a maximum contribution limit.

PAYE
(For Limited Companies & all full-time Employees)
PAYE stands for Pay-As-You-Earn and is Income Tax and NI (National Insurance) deducted by an employer from the employee's wage packet. You will also have to pay an employer's NI contribution. If you employ staff or are a limited company contact your nearest PAYE office (look under "Inland Revenue" in the Phone Book), and ask them for a "New Employers Starter Pack" which contains full instructions and forms. To see how PAYE works in practice, look at the worked example on pages 108 and 109.

Paying PAYE/NI   When you register for PAYE you will usually be sent a Payslip Booklet with instructions as to how to pay the tax. The amount due should cover both Income Tax and National Insurance, including the employers contribution. Most employers have to pay this monthly but if your monthly payments are below a certain threshold (see the **Tax Data Page** at the back of this book) you can elect to pay quarterly. For further advice, contact your PAYE office.

CORPORATION TAX
(For Limited Companies only)
This is a tax on the profits of a business in much the same way as Income Tax is calculated for a sole trader or partnership. Corporation Tax is normally paid 9 months after the end of the accounting year.

If as a Director you take a wage out of the company, the wage will be liable to Income Tax which will have to be deducted from your wage packet under the PAYE scheme mentioned above. Shareholders in the company can be paid "dividends" out of the profits of the company but the tax rules are complex with ACT (Advance Corporation Tax) having to be paid by the company – this requires your accountant's advice.

VALUE ADDED TAX (VAT)
First refer to the item on VAT at the end of the **Making it Legal** chapter. The VAT "bible" is the VAT Guide (Notice 700) which will tell you all you need to know about VAT. Remember that you do not need to register for VAT unless your taxable turnover exceeds (or is likely to exceed) a certain figure – see the **Tax Data Page**. Registration is also required if at any time it appears you will exceed the threshold in the next 30 days. If you need to register for VAT then you must keep additional records to those you would

Coping with Taxation

HOW VAT WORKS IN PRACTICE

This example assumes the VAT rate is 17.5%. Should this be changed the principle will remain the same but obviously the figures given in this example will be different.

A VAT-registered trader buys goods for £100 to which VAT at 17.5% is added so his bill is £117.50. The £17.50 is called his "input tax" which he can reclaim later. When he sells the goods he puts a mark-up on them and sells them for, let us say, £200. Since he is VAT-registered the £200 will include VAT (the actual amount is found by multiplying £200 by $7/47$ which is called the "VAT fraction" and it equals £29.79). The £29.79 is called his "output tax". When completing his VAT Return, on that one transaction he would owe £29.79 in VAT but he can reclaim £17.50, so the net amount he has to pay to Customs & Excise is:

$$£29.79 - £17.50 = £12.29.$$

Tip: One way to remember the VAT fraction of $7/47$ (when the VAT rate is 17.5%) is to think of a Boeing 747 Jumbo jet.

otherwise keep for the business. In particular you need to record all taxable goods and services that you buy and sell as part of the business. There is no set way to do this but your records must be such that you can fill in your VAT Return and done so a VAT inspector can understand them. Ask your accountant about this or your local VAT office. In addition as a VAT-registered trader you will have to give proper tax invoices unless you sell direct to the public in which case you only need to provide a tax invoice if requested. The VAT publication "Keeping Records and Accounts" gives more information and is very readable.

Note that as a VAT-registered trader you can normally only reclaim "input tax" if you have a proper tax invoice.

If you are registered for VAT then you must normally make a return to the Customs & Excise each quarter on a Form VAT 100 (usually referred to as the "VAT Return"). Refer to the specimen form opposite. You have one month from the end of the quarterly period to complete and return the form and to make your payment (if you owe VAT). If your "input tax" exceeds your "output tax" total, then once you have submitted your VAT Return you can expect a payment from HM Customs & Excise. Finally, do remember that there are stiff penalties for late submission of VAT Returns.

Tax Point An important aspect to remember when completing the VAT Return is the "Tax Point" (ie the date or "time of supply") of a transaction. In practice this is normally the date given on the invoice (provided the invoice is raised promptly) but note that legally this is only one of the possible relevant dates, ie when goods were supplied or a service completed are other possible Tax Points. Provided a Tax Point is within the quarter on which you are reporting then it has to be included in your VAT Return (even if no payment has yet been made!) unless you are using the "Cash Accounting Scheme".

Tax Invoices In general, a VAT invoice (usually called a "tax invoice") should have a unique identifying number and give the supplier's name, address and VAT number, the date the invoice is issued, the time of supply (ie tax point), the type of supply (eg sale or rental), a full description and quantity of the goods or services, the rate of cash discount offered (if any), the rate of VAT, the total (excluding VAT), the amount of VAT and the total payable. The invoice should also give the customer's name and address unless you mainly sell direct to the public and the invoice total is under a certain figure (currently £100).

If selling to other EC countries, the customer's VAT number and country code must appear on your invoice (in addition to your own VAT number with a GB prefix).

The "Cash Accounting Scheme" This special scheme allows a small business to account for VAT on the basis of payments received and made, rather than tax invoices issued and received. This can be a particular help if you give your customers long periods of credit.

The "Annual Accounting Scheme" Small businesses with a taxable turnover less than a certain threshold may be eligible to opt for this scheme whereby the business can account for its VAT by making regular interim payments then completing one annual VAT Return with a final payment, adjusted to balance the account.

KEY POINT For more information on these schemes and VAT in general, it is essential you contact HM Customs & Excise■

Value Added Tax Return
For the period
to

HM Customs and Excise

For Official Use

SPECIMEN

Fold | Here

Registration number

Period

You could be liable to a financial penalty if your completed return and all the VAT payable are not received by the due date.

Due date:

For official use D O R only

Before you fill in this form please read the notes on the back and the VAT leaflet *"Filling in your VAT return"*. Fill in all boxes clearly in ink, and write 'none' where necessary. Don't put a dash or leave any box blank. If there are no pence write "00" in the pence column. **Do not** enter more than one amount in any box.

For official use			£	p
	VAT due in this period on **sales** and other outputs	1		
	VAT due in this period on **acquisitions** from other **EC Member States**	2		
	Total VAT due **(the sum of boxes 1 and 2)**	3		
	VAT reclaimed in this period on **purchases** and other inputs (including acquisitions from the EC)	4		
	Net VAT to be paid to Customs or reclaimed by you **(Difference between boxes 3 and 4)**	5		
	Total value of **sales** and all other outputs excluding any VAT. **Include your box 8 figure**	6		00
	Total value of **purchases** and all other inputs excluding any VAT. **Include your box 9 figure**	7		00
	Total value of all **supplies** of goods and related services, excluding any VAT, to other **EC Member States**	8		00
	Total value of all **acquisitions** of goods and related services, excluding any VAT, from other **EC Member States**	9		00

Retail schemes. If you have used any of the schemes in the period covered by this return, enter the relevant letter(s) in this box.

If you are enclosing a payment please tick this box.

DECLARATION: You, or someone on your behalf, must sign below.

I, ...declare that the
(Full name of signatory in BLOCK LETTERS)

information given above is true and complete.

Signature ....Date ....19 ....

A false declaration can result in prosecution.

VAT 100 (Full)

PCU (June 1996)

VAT 100 (One side only shown here, reduced in size). H.M. Customs & Excise form.
Crown Copyright. Reproduced with the permission of the Controller of HMSO.

107

PAYE WORKED EXAMPLE (Fictitious Employer & Employee)

Deductions Working Sheet P11   Year to 5 April 19 **98**

Employer's name **WORTHLESS PRODUCTS**

Tax Office and reference

Employee's surname in CAPITALS **SMITH**   First two forenames **JOHN**

National Insurance no.

Date of birth in figures Day **29** Month **02** Year **70**

Works no. etc

Date of starting in figures Day **06** Month **05** Year **97**

Date of leaving in figures Day Month Year

Tax code † **404L**   Amended code †   Wk/Mth in which applied

National Insurance contributions

For guidance on National Insurance and the completion of columns 1a to 1h see CWG1 'Employer's Quick Guide to Pay As You Earn and National Insurance Contributions' - card 9
For guidance on Statutory Sick Pay figures see leaflet CA30
For guidance on Statutory Maternity Pay figures see leaflet CA29
or contact the Employers Help Line - telephone number is in the CWG1

At the top of each section in the NI Tables there is a letter, for example A, B, C, D or E. Copy that letter from the Table you use to the box bottom left overleaf - see ▼ overleaf. If the employee's circumstances change part way through a year the letter may change as well. Record all letters with separate totals for each table letter used.
Remember to record under letter Y any Class 1A on the last line of the box at ▼.
See the CWG1 card 11 for further information and examples

PAYE Income Tax

For guidance on completing this form see CWG1 'Employer's Quick Guide to Pay As You Earn and National Insurance Contributions'
- Card 10 for general completion
- Card 12 specifically for K codes
- Cards 11 and 12 for examples using suffix and K codes

Earnings recorded in Column 1a should not exceed the Upper Earnings Limit

1a £	1b £	1c £	Month no	Week no	1 £	Total pay to date £	4a £	4b £	5 £	6 £	7 £	NET WAGE
				1								
				2								
				3								
			1	4	728.00		79.45					
222	39.54	17.29		5	222 950.00 389.35			560.65 116.97			37.52	167.19

(table columns: 1a, 1b, 1c, 1d, 1e, 1f, 1g, 1h, Month no, Week no, 1, Total pay to date, 4a, 4b, 5, 6, 6a, 6b, 7, 8, NET WAGE)

† If amended cross out previous code.
✓ If any week/month the amount in column 4a is more than the amount in column 3, leave column 5 blank.

P11(1997)   BMSD8/96

Assume you need to work out the net pay for a new employee, John Smith. First prepare a Deductions Working Sheet (as shown above) using the information on Smith's Form P45, such as the £728 and £79.45 (if Smith had no P45, refer to the PAYE P8 Guide). On his first pay day (9th May), assume Smith's gross wage is £222.

Now open the *National Insurance Not contracted-out contributions Tables 1* (see top Table extract opposite) and enter the following on the Deductions Working Sheet:

Col 1a   Insert Smith's earnings on which he pays National Insurance contributions (£222).

Cols 1b/1c From Table A get the £39.54 and £17.29.

Col 2   Insert Smith's gross pay (£222) in this column.

Col 3   Insert the total pay Smith has had to date (£950).

Now Open the *Pay Adjustment Tables* at Week 5 (middle opposite).

Col 4   As Smith's Tax Code is 404L (taken from his P45), his total "free pay" to date is £389.35.

Col 5   Now deduct £389.35 from £950 = £560.65.

Next, refer to the *Taxable Pay Tables* (bottom Table opposite).

Col 6   The tax due on £560 is £115 + £13.80 = £128.80 less £11.83 (from the Subtraction Table (not shown here but is found beside Table B) and is due to the 20% tax band).

Col 7   Take £79.45 from £116.97 to get the tax due: £37.52.

NET WAGE   From Smith's gross wage of £222, deduct the National Insurance (£17.29) and Income Tax (£37.52) = **£167.19**.

Important Note: Always consult the PAYE P8 Guide and note that Tax Codes and Tables change from time to time.

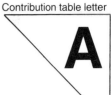

Weekly table

Earnings on which employee's contributions payable 1a	Total of employee's and employer's contributions payable 1b	Employee's contributions payable 1c	Employer's contributions ▼	Earnings on which employee's contributions payable 1a	Total of employee's and employer's contributions payable 1b	Employee's contributions payable 1c	Employer's contributions ▼
£	£	£	£	£	£	£	£
182	26.06	13.29	**12.77**	222	39.54	17.29	**22.25**
183	26.23	13.39	**12.84**	223	39.74	17.39	**22.35**

TABLE A - PAY ADJUSTMENT — Week 5 — May 4 to May 10

Code	Total pay adjustment to date	Code	Total pay adjustment to date	Code	Total pay adjustment to date	Code	Total pay adjustment to date	Code	Total pay adjustment to date	Code	Total pay adjustment to date	Code	Total pay adjustment to date	Code	Total pay adjustment to date	Code	Total pay adjustment to date
	£		£		£		£		£		£		£		£		£
0	NIL																
1	1.85	61	59.55	121	117.25	181	174.95	241	232.60	301	290.30	351	338.40	401	386.45	451	434.55
2	2.80	62	60.50	122	118.20	182	175.90	242	233.60	302	291.25	352	339.35	402	387.45	452	435.50
3	3.75	63	61.45	123	119.15	183	176.85	243	234.55	303	292.25	353	340.30	403	388.40	453	436.45
4	4.75	64	62.45	124	120.10	184	177.80	244	235.50	304	293.20	354	341.25	404	389.35	454	437.45
5	5.70	65	63.40	125	121.10	185	178.75	245	236.45	305	294.15	355	342.25	405	390.30	455	438.40

Pages 2 and 3 tell you when to use these tables

Table B
(Tax at 23%)

Remember to use the Subtraction Tables on Page 7

Tax Due on Taxable Pay from £1 to £99

Total TAXABLE PAY to date	Total TAX DUE to date	Total TAXABLE PAY to date	Total TAX DUE to date
£	£	£	£
1	0.23	56	12.88
2	0.46	57	13.11
3	0.69	58	13.34
4	0.92	59	13.57
5	1.15	60	13.80

Tax Due on Taxable Pay from £100 to £26,100

Total TAXABLE PAY to date	Total TAX DUE to date	Total TAXABLE PAY to date	Total TAX DUE to date	Total TAXABLE PAY to date	Total TAX DUE to date	Total TAXABLE PAY to date	Total TAX DUE to date
£	£	£	£	£	£	£	£
100	23.00	6600	1518.00	13100	3013.00	19600	4508.00
200	46.00	6700	1541.00	13200	3036.00	19700	4531.00
300	69.00	6800	1564.00	13300	3059.00	19800	4554.00
400	92.00	6900	1587.00	13400	3082.00	19900	4577.00
500	115.00	7000	1610.00	13500	3105.00	20000	4600.00
600	138.00	7100	1633.00	13600	3128.00	20100	4623.00

Form P11 (Opposite) and excerpts from Contributions Agency and Inland Revenue **Tables** (above). Shown here reduced in size.
Crown Copyright. Reproduced with the permission of the Controller of HMSO.

Solving a Cashflow Problem

T HIS is a situation that can confront many businesses, especially new ones, and if it is not handled correctly it might lead to the premature demise of the venture. The term "a cashflow problem" can cover a variety of ailments but the net effect is the business runs out of money so bills cannot be met. Newish businesses with their up-front launch costs and lowish initial sales are particularly vulnerable.

Detection

First of all, you have to be aware that there is a problem as this may not be so obvious in its early stages, particularly if accounts books are not fully up to date as everyone has been "too busy". One of the best early indicators is a Cashflow Forecast which is continually failing to meet its forecasts.

How to do a Cashflow Forecast and Cashflow Management techniques are covered in detail in earlier chapters.

If you did a "break-even" Cashflow Forecast where your predicted sales just match your outgoings and then found that the actual trading results were falling below these thresholds, you would know that the business is heading towards a major cashflow problem.

In any business, sales go through peaks and troughs which may be seasonal in character but with a properly prepared Cashflow Forecast it will still be possible to spot a problem.

If nothing is done the situation will deteriorate and one or a number of classic warning signals may become evident. These are:
1. A rising overdraft level (without any specific reason).
2. Increasing difficulties in paying trade creditors.
3. Falling behind in the monthly PAYE and National Insurance payments.

These are all very serious signs of impending disaster and they demand immediate action.

A Survival Strategy

Once a looming cashflow problem is detected, you must move fast as the business will be growing weaker and there will be less time to make changes and fewer options available. But what should you do?

People tend to react to this situation in two ways, either completely ignoring the problem as they simply cannot face up to it (and they may be unsure what to do)

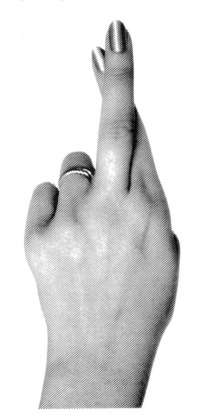

Simply crossing your fingers will not help!

or they over react and institute panic measures which are ill-considered and potentially damaging. In most peoples' minds questions may fly around – should they advertise more? Should they cut their prices? Should they sack their staff?

The only sensible course of action is first to analyse the situation you are in, second to consider the options, third to draw up some sort of plan and finally to try to carry it out. It sounds simple, but of course it's not. However, you must try, and the sooner, the better.

The first thing you must do is to work out how to give yourself some time. When a business is not going smoothly the demands on you can increase, making it very difficult to find "thinking" time. But if the business is facing a crisis you simply **must** make time. A practical suggestion is to set aside half an hour before you start work each day to concentrate your full energy on the problem (as most people are more alert in the morning and the day's dramas have not yet intruded). The next steps are as follows:

Step 1: Find Out How Bad It Is!

It is vital to get a complete and up-to-date financial picture. A Cashflow Forecast should be prepared quickly together with lists of all outstanding creditors (ie those people you owe money to) and debtors (who are those people who owe you money) and a further note or list of orders or sales likely to materialise in the next few weeks or months.

Step 2: Reduce Your Outgoings

The business is running out of cash so the next step is to reduce the outgoings until it matches income. This might require quite drastic action. It may involve reducing staffing levels, getting out of expensive rented premises and generally cutting back wherever it may be possible.

KEY POINT If you cannot or will not match outgoings to income then you will ultimately run out of cash. It is as simple as that!

Step 3: Tackle The Root Cause
With the first two steps carried out, you can now turn your attention to tackling the root cause of the problem. It is important to identify clearly which factor or factors are relevant in your own case – it may be fairly self-evident! Let us look at each one in turn.

> In general, cashflow problems may occur due to either one, or worse, a combination of five main factors:
>
> 1. **Sales Levels** – too low.
> 2. **Overheads** – too high.
> 3. **Profit Margins** – too small.
> 4. **Debtor Payments** – too slow.
> 5. **Trading Level** – too great.

TACKLING THE PROBLEM

SALES LEVELS TOO LOW

Having too low a turnover is a common problem with new (ie under 2-3 years old) small businesses and there are several reasons for this. Many new businesses are set up with a lot of optimism, but insufficient knowledge of the market and too little capital. Another major factor is that it takes time, often a great deal of time (ie years, not months), to become established and this period is normally much longer than most initial Business Plans allow.

The problem is, of course, that sales during this early period can be lower than that required to support the business (and give you a living wage). So what are your options?

Option 1: Improve Your Marketing
There is hardly a business in existence which at one time or another has not presented its proprietors or Directors with the task of how to increase sales to rectify a cashflow problem.

The first task is to identify the main reason why sales levels are low. A low turnover means too few customers and/ or each customer is spending too little. Look carefully at each step in the selling process as covered below.

In all this work, write down notes on your thoughts and conclusions. This is really most important for if just left "in the head" it can all get very confusing and contradictory.

1. Finding Customers   Ask yourself how you expect people to hear about your new business and then try asking some how they actually heard about you. Also, work out roughly how many people need to hear about you to produce sufficient enquiries that eventually lead to enough sales to support your business.

Many small businesses promote themselves inadequately due to lack of time, money (and possibly expertise). But simply deciding to "spend more on advertising" is unlikely to be the right answer and in any event your business may not be able to afford much advertising in its present condition. It is better to listen to your existing customers who you are serving so you can improve this vital aspect.

As a simple rule-of-thumb, if your customers are "trade", then direct approach by phone or letter followed up by a meeting is likely to give the best results. With consumers, the task is a little more difficult (unless you are opening a shop) and the precise approach will require careful thought. As an example, if you are launching a grass cutting and gardening business, you might put leaflets through letter-boxes and then follow up in person.

KEY POINT Increased advertising is unlikely to yield sufficient returns at this stage.

2. Stimulating Customer Interest   It may be that sufficient customers are aware of you but their interest has not been caught. Your company or its products or services may not look up-to-date enough, or they may look too up-market or too down-market, for most of your potential customers.

Your leaflet, shop window or adverts may either be confusing to potential customers or the people may simply not realise just what you can offer (this is a very common problem!). Try speaking to people who are *not* making a purchase – their answers could be highly illuminating. Something else you can do is to look at the competition – what are they doing successfully which you are not?

3. Satisfying Customer Needs   Take a moment to pencil a brief note comparing your product or service with your competitors. Maybe you include a feature which is putting off potential buyers or missing a feature which your competitors are offering. Though, of course, your competitors may not be right either!

Your business may be projecting one image but the bulk of your stock may be more suitable for a different image, so

Solving a Cashflow Problem

you attract customers but cannot satisfy their needs.

Price is often of crucial importance in a number of trade sectors, so ensure your pricing is correct, but just dropping the price is not necessarily a good idea, as a low price may send the wrong message, ie it may imply that what you are offering is somehow cheap or of low quality. Again, talking to people will shed more light on this aspect.

O╌ Don't be panicked into simply dropping your prices!
KEY POINT

4. Making The Sale Sometimes the product or service is right, the customer is ready to make the purchase but the actual sales technique being used is simply inadequate or even off-putting. Not everyone is a good, natural salesperson and selling does require its own persuasive skills, knowledge and enthusiasm even when the product or service is itself excellent.

If any one of the four steps above is not quite right, that is where to concentrate your initial efforts. If all the steps in the selling process are genuinely being done *reasonably* well (and there is little point in kidding yourself if this is not the case) then the truth may be there is insufficient demand for your product or service as it currently stands. In that case you might consider the next option:

Option 2: Modify Your Business
In many cases your analysis of the problem of low sales will reveal several areas that need improving but it may also show that you need to modify what you are offering to make it more sale-able. Due to your cashflow predicament

there may be a temptation to do something really drastic in terms of changing the product or service on offer, but it is probably much safer to stick to what you are doing and to make a number of fine adjustments and check the response to each of those. These small changes can be implemented much quicker, at much lower cost and involve much lower risk.

O╌ Any changes needed should be *evolutionary* rather than *revolutionary*.
KEY POINT

In terms of what changes to make, try to recall what questions, criticisms, suggestions or short-comings were voiced by would-be customers. This is where your inspiration should come from.

Option 3: Diversify
It may be that your initial market research was not quite spot-on and the market is really looking for a completely different product or service, or a major adaptation of what you are currently offering. This is not an unusual situation. However, calm consideration needs to be given to this option as change or diversification on this scale must be thought of as akin to an entirely new project, almost like setting up a new venture from scratch. Thus it will take time and money to establish and may mean venturing into unchartered waters.

Diversification should not be seen as a panacea to your current problems, however it can be very successful if carried out with due market research and especially if it is allied to what the business is currently doing, thereby building on the contacts and business knowledge which have already been acquired.

Brain-Storming To come up with a diversified product or service, try a "brain-storming" session. To do this, get away from the work environment and take your fellow partners, Directors, key staff or other confidant(e)s. You could probably use a sitting room in one of your homes, provided it is large enough and peaceful, or if that is not suitable, hire a small function room in a local Hotel. Ensure that lots of coffee and sandwiches are on hand and that there are absolutely no interruptions.

The session should start in the morning when everyone is fresh and it may last until mid or even late afternoon. The "rules" of the session are that people come up with as many ideas as they can but are never criticised or ridiculed by the others, however wild an idea may seem at first. This tends to encourage the more unusual ideas and some lateral thinking.

If there are more than three or four people in the group it might also be useful to have a large piece of paper or flip-chart which everyone can see and on which all the ideas are written.

After a few hours the group can switch from generating fresh ideas to looking in more detail at those already thrown up and by the end of the session there should be a number of ideas to be followed up as "possibles". All these ideas should be recorded, in brief, for any future sessions or discussions.

OVERHEADS TOO HIGH
When you start any business you purchase stock, buy equipment, maybe rent premises and perhaps take on staff, all on the not unreasonable assumption that sales will be made, cash will flow in and these overheads can be sustained. However, if sales are

lower than expected you will soon run out of cash. See the box – right.

A totally avoidable cause of cashflow problems is caused by the proprietors or Directors simply drawing out from the business too much cash for themselves. This is sometimes because no thought has been given to make any provision to pay tax, VAT etc.

PROFIT MARGINS TOO SMALL

Margins may be lower than anticipated for a variety of reasons – the need to discount heavily (possibly due to competition or demanded by a large customer); rises in raw material or stock costs which cannot be passed on immediately to customers or exchange rate fluctuations (when you import or export).

Another problem is that even though you may be making sales at your full normal price, these prices may themselves be too low, allowing inadequate margin to sustain the business. Refer to the chapter **Marketing and Sales** again.

Many businesses offer a variety of products and services which have different profit margins. This gives them the opportunity to switch slowly from low margin work to that which has the higher margins. This simple and gentle change in marketing strategy may mean a temporary decrease in turnover but an increase in overall profitability of the business, especially if overheads are reduced to match the initially lower level of trading.

Another point to note is that even if your margins are typical for your trade, you should always work at increasing them by a few percentage points here and there, wherever possible, as cumulatively this can add up to a useful increase in profit.

HINTS TO KEEP DOWN OVERHEADS (& OTHER EXPENSES)

Staff: Only take on staff when you have to and minimise staffing needs by investing in automation (eg computers). Eliminate all unnecessary work. Simplify work practices! It may be better to have one high calibre employee who needs less supervision than several of lesser ability. Try to increase productivity by tight control, comprehensive job descriptions, proper training and realistic incentives. More mature and experienced part-time staff can be particularly worthwhile. Alternatively try contracting out parts of your work to other companies or use freelancers. PS: If you plan to make staff redundant, get professional advice first.

Vehicles: Consider which way to finance the purchase as there are big differences in costs. Buy nearly new, rather than new. Mileage costs money so consider using routeplanner software to minimise journeys (and save your valuable time).

Premises: This can be another major overhead, especially in retailing where a prime site is usually vital. Rent as little space as you can squeeze into (as everything is valued in £/sqft). Challenge rent reviews. Query rating levels. Consider purchasing rather than renting as one is an investment, the other merely an expense (provided you buy wisely).

Heat & Light: We insulate our homes but seem less interested in doing this with our workplace and therefore waste energy.

Insurances: Check you are not over- insured and get alternative quotes.

Purchasing: Approve all purchases yourself especially while funds are tight.

Travel: If you use trains, planes or hotels, research the different fare options, as considerable savings are possible.

Finance: What interest rates are you paying? Investigate the best way to fund your venture. Generally an overdraft is the cheapest way. Borrowing too much is called "over-gearing" and can cripple a business, especially if times get hard or interest rates rise. Excessive stock levels are one cause of high borrowings. Aim to be financially self-sufficient, ie have no borrowings. *Tip:* To avoid bank charges on business cheques, use your personal credit card where possible then pay off each month using one business cheque.

Advertising & Promotion: Assess if what you are doing is generating sufficient sales to cover their costs, and don't be surprised if they are not!

Phone Bills: These are almost always larger than necessary! Try to reduce the number of long chatty calls by using faxes or e-mail. These can also be transmitted at cheaper phone times.

Sundries: Expenses lumped together under this general heading can cover a multitude of sins, analysis of which often causes a few surprises (and savings).

Solving a Cashflow Problem

DEBTOR PAYMENTS TOO SLOW

Slow payment by customers (or worse, non-payment) is a business malady we regrettably seem to have to learn to live with and almost every business needs to spend time pursuing bad payers. New, small businesses are particularly vulnerable as they are often under-capitalised and in their eagerness to get a sale or win a contract may turn a blind eye to the credit-worthiness of the buyer. The situation is aggravated by some larger companies who use their suppliers as a flexible (and free) source of credit finance!

If you already have a problem with bad payers a suggested Debt Recovery strategy as outlined in the box below might be considered but the important point is to minimise future exposure to such risks. Proper credit checks should be carried out on all customers requiring credit over a threshold you feel relevant, for instance it may not be worth the effort in a trade-to-trade context proving credit worthiness if your maximum exposure per customer is under, say £50. Credit checks should include the customer's bank and at least two other suppliers. Whereas the bank can give an indication of the *ability* of the company to pay, the other suppliers will give a clue as to their *willingness* to pay!

Private consumers do not usually expect credit, whereas trade customers invariably expect 30 days minimum.

Getting paid by overseas customers can present different and sometimes very difficult problems. Refer to the chapter **Exporting** earlier in this book.

KEY POINT The almost irresistible temptation to take a big order from an unproven and possible credit risk customer should always be avoided.

Credit Checks If a potential customer is a limited company, you can get a copy of their annual accounts for about £6 from Companies House (see page 17 for addresses). In addition to doing your own credit checks, you might also use a reputable credit checking agency, such as Dun & Bradstreet (Tel: 01494 423242) who provide a very detailed credit report for around £55 plus VAT.

Risk Reduction Other ways to reduce your exposure include spreading the risk, ie more small customers rather than several big ones (though your administration time rises dramatically); payment by pro-forma invoice (ie payment in advance); taking a deposit; splitting larger orders into several smaller deliveries each of which has to be paid before the next part of the order is despatched; and, where appropriate, the use of Factoring (see opposite).

TRADING LEVEL TOO GREAT

Another situation when a cashflow problem can appear is when a company is expanding more rapidly than its available working capital allows. Called "over-trading", this situation therefore affects businesses that could be regarded as successful.

The business obviously has to either slow down or have more capital injected into it. (Note: Some of the comments on Re-Financing below do not strictly apply to a company that is over-trading).

RE-FINANCING

Sometimes businesses faced with cash-flow problems try to "remedy" them by looking for more cash to finance their increasing debt. The danger is, of course, self-evident in that the problem will not go away unless the root causes are tackled. However, even tackling these will often require some re-financing or financial restructuring.

This situation faces many businesses and it is not an easy task – there are probably few assets; the business may already be up to its maximum overdraft limit and its creditors may be knocking on the door for their money.

The first step is to decide on a pre-ferred course of action and its cost. A contingency factor should be allowed

---

A DEBT RECOVERY STRATEGY

When you complete the job . .	Send Invoice promptly (and specify payment due date)
At the end of the month	Send Statement
2 weeks after payment due . .	Phone customer (Accounts Dept) taking contact's name
1-2 weeks later	Phone same person asking why the delay?
1-2 weeks later	Send polite letter by "Recorded Delivery"
1 week later still	Phone the Boss, asking if they have a problem?
Within a week or two	If possible, visit in person, or send a more direct letter
When?	Consider Small Claims Court (but take advice first)

Solving a Cashflow Problem

for, since if insufficient funds are raised it is most unlikely that you could re-finance again while the business is still in trouble. You only get one chance!

As the business is still trading, there are some things in its favour: its main creditors will normally want to see the business continuing to trade and get over its problems. They have a vested interest in the venture which is more than just the immediate money it owes them. In addition, the Bank Manager does not want a failed business on his or her career record; trade suppliers will want to retain the "account" for the future, and Landlords do not want the expense of finding a new tenant. None of these people want the problems of the inevitable paperwork they will be faced with if your business actually fails especially if it ceases trading still owing them money. However, if they believe there is little hope in saving the situation they will probably just cut their losses, and close you down.

Many people put off telling their creditors that they are running into problems. This is quite natural but unfortunately, being kept in the dark, the creditors may panic. So one needs to talk, guardedly, to them all. They may even wish to see something in writing.

A Rescue Plan   A letter can outline your plan. It should confidently and clearly explain how you intend to correct the situation with their support. The plan should set modest goals – for any failure to meet goals will be seen as a failure of the whole plan, with dire consequences. The letter should be brief, though your banker (who knows your accounts any-way) will probably need more details. Any promises of repayments should be on modest timescales as they will lose confidence if any repayment is missed or late.

Two precautions must be stressed: a) you should not divulge any more of your business details than are absolutely essential and b) you must assume who-ever you speak to will take whatever action is in *their* best interest not yours. If this presents a potential risk to you then only proceed with caution and first take impartial and professional advice.

KEY POINT Any rescue plan should set modest goals that you can confidently meet.

Banks   These will often refuse further cash (in the form of a loan or larger over-draft) unless new capital, possibly equal to the bank's increased risk, is introduced into the business.   For instance, if £10,000 is needed then the bank is unlikely to agree to more than about £5,000 with the balance being new capital injected by some other party. This cash may come from one or a number of sources, such as the sale of some personal effects, re-mortgaging one's home, finding a new partner or share-holder or a loan from a friend.

Sometimes where your product or service is unique and vital to the smooth operation of a larger company who is a major customer of yours, that company may be prepared to make a loan (with interest) to keep you going, or to purchase a share-holding in your business. It can be a good method if the circumstances are right.

Factoring

For those non-retail businesses with a cashflow problem due to rapid expansion and where the turnover is already £100K plus, then one option to consider is factoring (also called "sales-linked funding" or "cashflow financing").

In this method, when you send an invoice to your customer, you send a copy of the invoice to the factor, who then pays you typically 75% of the invoice total almost immediately. The factor then takes the responsibility for chasing the debt, issuing statements and reminders. Your invoice is anno-tated that the amount should be paid to the factor and not yourself. When your customer pays, you receive the balance from the factor (less their charges).

Factoring costs are broadly compar-able with the cost of a bank overdraft, but has the advantages of faster pay-ment and the factor has the problem of chasing the debt.

Insufficient financial control . . . .?

FURTHER READING Please also refer to: "**The Greatest Sales & Marketing Book**" – see the end of this book for more details■

115

Getting more Business Advice

THERE are many people who can help you with your business. In alphabetical order, these include:

Accountants   An accountant is an essential part of your team. Accountants vary greatly in their abilities and in the time they are prepared to spend with each client – so choose carefully! An initial meeting with an accountant is usually free. Discuss your business plans, what accounts books you plan to keep and ask for an indication of likely annual fees. An accountant should always be consulted when setting up a business and later to help you with your annual Tax Return. It is important that you get on with your accountant and keep in touch.

Bank Managers   A Bank Manager's advice is usually free and you should keep them abreast of all developments and plans. They are careful people so do not frighten them with sudden changes of course and do not give them ultimatums such as "If I don't get the £5,000 overdraft by tomorrow, I shall have to lay off my staff . . ." Give them warning. You should phone, visit or write to your bank manager every few months just to keep in touch. Many bankers have more business knowledge than you might expect, but as with any service if you are unhappy with your bank, then consider changing branch or to another bank.

Business Links   It can be very confusing to know which business support agency to approach. In England, to solve this problem, some 240 Business Links have been created. They will answer your queries or put you in touch with the right people. The Business Links are a partnership of TECs, Chambers of Commerce, local authorities, local enterprise agencies and others.

Business Shops   These are "first-stop" shops around Scotland. Information and guidance is available on subjects such as start-up, training, export, legal matters, franchising, marketing, finance etc.

Chartered Surveyors   Always use a chartered surveyor when purchasing premises or taking on a lease (ie renting). They can check on the physical condition of the building, advise if the rent or purchase price is fair and they can check and advise on the lease conditions and planning permission. They will charge for their service so ask them for an estimate beforehand.

Enterprise Agencies   These are usually funded jointly by the local private and public sectors which allows them to provide many of their services free. The objective of the several hundred Enterprise Agencies is to encourage new and existing small businesses, providing mainly free business advice and much more besides. To find your nearest, look in the Yellow Pages.

Government Tax Offices   Don't forget that many of your straightforward tax queries can be answered by the appropriate tax office – Inland Revenue, Contributions Agency or Customs & Excise (VAT Offices).

Industrial Development Units   Many local authorities have such units. They can provide business advice and usually have workshops and factory premises to rent. They can also advise on local planning and licencing matters.

Insurance Brokers   Most businesses need insurance of some sort and in certain situations (eg if you employ anyone) insurance is a legal requirement, so a good registered broker is worth approaching before you start.

Local Enterprise Companies (LECs)   These are business-led organisations in Scotland, formed to encourage enterprise, provide training and assist small firms, in addition to other related activities. Get the address of your own LEC from Yellow Pages.

Solicitors   A good solicitor is needed when setting up a business, taking over premises or whenever you have legal queries. Remember that thinking ahead and getting good advice early can prevent bigger problems later on.

Training and Enterprise Councils (TECs)   These are business-led organisations in England and Wales, formed to encourage enterprise, provide training and assist small firms, in addition to other related activities. Get the address of your own TEC from a Jobcentre or Yellow Pages.

And Finally   Advice can never be a substitute for decision making! Collect all the advice you can but in the end you must make your own decisions■

Tax Data Page

Income Tax

Lower Rate: 20% (for that portion of taxable income below £4,100)
Basic Rate: 23%
Higher Rate: 40% (for that portion of taxable income exceeding £26,100)

Personal Allowances:

Single Person:	£4,045
Married Couple or Additional Personal Allowance:	£1,830 extra *(but relief is restricted to 15%)*

PAYE: If an employer's average total monthly PAYE payment is below a certain figure, then they can usually opt to pay their PAYE quarterly rather than monthly. Contact the Inland Revenue for details.

Simple Tax Accounts: For Sole Traders or Partnerships, if their annual turnover is below £15,000, in the appropriate part of the SELF ASSESSMENT Tax Return, instead of providing a detailed breakdown of income and expenses, the Inland Revenue simply requires a total of: (1) turnover, (2) allowable business expenses and (3) the net profits.

National Insurance

Class 1 (Employees/Directors) — Lower Limit: £62 weekly or £269 monthly, ie there is normally no National Insurance contribution (or an Employers contribution) on earnings below this limit.

Class 1A (Cars and Fuel) — This is a contribution (only by Employers) if company cars are made available for private use to their Employees or Directors.

Class 2 (Sole Traders/Partners) — £6.15 per week. (The Small Earnings Exception limit is £3,480 per annum).

Class 4 (Sole Traders/Partners) — Calculated as 6% of profits between £7,010 and £24,180, ie no Class 4 contribution is due if taxable profits are under £7,010.

Corporation Tax
(Limited Companies only)

The tax rate is 21% for profits up to £300,000. This is called the "small companies' rate". Thereafter the tax rate is on a sliding scale up to 31% for profits of £1.5M.

Value Added Tax (VAT)

Standard Rate: 17½%   Registration threshold: £49,000 (turnover)

Capital Gains Tax (CGT)

Annual exemption: First £6,500 of chargeable gain.

INDEX

Great Books For Small Business . . .

The Greatest Sales & Marketing Book
The Practical Action Guide for a Small Business

Full of ideas to increase your sales. How to advertise successfully. Many worked examples, eg Pricing, a Press Release and Leaflet. Tips to survive a Recession. Advice to keep down overheads. Market Research – how to do it and how it helps. Excellent reviews in, for example, *The Times, Money Week* and *British Business* magazine. 120 pages and highly illustrated. 3rd Edition.

By **Peter Hingston**   ISBN 0 906555 17 5   **£7.50**

The Greatest Guide to Home-based Business
101 Great Business Ideas plus How to Work from Home

Working from home is the growth area of new businesses in the 1990s. In addition to advice on starting a business, it covers the particular problems of working from home. The book also features 101 stimulating business ideas to inspire the reader. 120 pages and illustrated. 2nd Edition.

By **Peter Hingston & Eric Smith**   ISBN 0 906555 19 1   **£8.50**

The Best Accounts Books
For non-VAT (and VAT) registered Small Businesses

These accounts books, launched in 1991, are now used by tens of thousands of businesses around the UK. Written in layman's language, with a simple and attractive format and full instructions. Suitable for most businesses (sole traders, partnerships or limited companies). There are two books for non-VAT registered businesses and one for a VAT business. Pages from these accounts books are illustrated in this book (p97 and p100-102). A4 size, hardcover.

The YELLOW BOOK (for a **cash** business)   ISBN 0 906555 11 6   **£8.99**

The BLUE BOOK (for a **credit** business)   ISBN 0 906555 12 4   **£8.99**

The BLUE VAT BOOK (VAT version)   ISBN 0 906555 14 0   **£10.99**

Please phone if you are in any doubt as to which book you should order.

The Best Small Business Accounts Software

The software mimics the non-VAT accounts books above. Suitable for any PC (not Apple Mac). Specify YELLOW or BLUE version. Supplied on 3½″ disk and available by Mail Order only. The price includes (limited) phone support. Easy!   **£39**

HOW TO ORDER

From a Bookshop: Quote them the ISBN number above and ask them to order the book [not software] from us through Teleordering. We usually despatch within 2-3 days. Trade terms.

Mail Order: For books, either phone us with your credit card details, or send a cheque made to "Hingston Publishing Co.", adding **£1.90** for p&p for 1 book (**£2.90** for 2 or 3 books). Allow 7-10 days for delivery. For software, please phone. Please note prices may change.

Hingston Publishing Co., Conifer House, 14 Ainslie Close, Hereford HR1 1JH, U.K.

Tel: 01432 344693   or   e-mail: hingston.publishing@btinternet.com